bobby dale

Have I Got a Song for You!

The Bobby Dale Story—
from juvenile delinquent on the streets to the Rock and Roll Hall of Fame

by Lou Waters

Printed in USA by

1094 New DeHaven Street, Suite 100
West Conshohocken, PA 19428-2713
Info@buybooksontheweb.com
www.buybooksontheweb.com
Toll-free (877) BUY BOOK
Local Phone (610) 941-9999
Fax (610) 941-9959

First Edition
2 3 4 5 6 7 8 9 10

Published by Lou Waters
email: louwaters@comcast.net
web: www.haveigotasongforyou.com

Library of Congress Cataloging-in-Publication Data

Waters, Lou

Have I Got a Song for You!
The Bobby Dale Story—
from juvenile delinquent on the streets
to the Rock and Roll Hall of Fame.
by Lou Waters
p.cm.
ISBN 0-7414-5616-8

Graphic Design & Typography
Tom Morin/Context Design Inc.
Galisteo, New Mexico
www.contextdesign.com

This book is dedicated to Normi, Joey and Tommy Dale and to the Bastiensen family.

Contents

Bobby Dale found his voice by sitting alone in a room behind a microphone.

Introduction

Rock 'n Roll Radio was purely an American invention of ingenious design. The origins of the music, to which it owed its historic success, can be traced to the early years of the twentieth century. The words "rockin' and rollin'" were heard in recorded music in 1916.

By 1956 rock 'n roll radio had become a social phenomenon that shaped the future of enormous numbers of young people around the world. The music was a fusion of rhythm and blues, black and white gospel, jazz and country western.

Teenagers coming of age danced, dated and lived their lives to the tunes of Chuck Berry, The Everly Brothers, The Drifters, Bobby Bland, Marty Robbins and Fats Domino. They crowned a "King" named Elvis and declared their independence from parents who were deeply disturbed by what they perceived as the sexual and tribal nature of the music.

Radio's nod to "popular music" in the 40's became an explosive force in the 50's that spread like wildfire as creative competition among radio stations vied for the attention of an audience that couldn't get enough of rock 'n roll. In every major market – the Top 40 station was the most listened to station. America became the land of "Top 40 formats": play the hits, hype the contests, give away huge sums of money and create excitement with the most talented disc jockeys you could find. The jocks made it happen. They were the ribbon on the exciting package that was to shape a generation.

Bobby Dale was one of those disc jockeys whose ambition in life was to avoid work at all costs. His teenage life of petty crime, reform school at 16, hard drinking and one serious brush with the law prepared him for a legendary career in radio that earned him a spot in Rock 'n Roll's Hall of Fame.

Bobby, on his father's lap, was "The Babe."

1

The Class of 1949

"South Minneapolis in the 1940's."

Growing up in South Minneapolis in the 1940's required a keen sense of self preservation. It was an uncertain and often dangerous time. The depression and world war left deep anxieties, financial potholes and uncertain futures for families and communities scrambling for their share of the American dream.

The family of Robert "Bobby" Dale Bastiensen were the have nots – only they didn't know it. "For a family that didn't have any money, I managed to be spoiled. My nickname was Babe all through junior and senior high school. That's what they called me, Babe," Bobby said.

Robert Dale Bastiensen was the youngest of six in a Norwegian immigrant family. His father, Erling worked the ore boats in the Great Lakes and was gone for months at a stretch. His mother, Sigrid was an upstairs maid at Pillsbury House. Neither could speak English when they first arrived in this country. Two of Bobby's older brothers were casualties of the war. One was seriously injured; another was killed in an air crash. The Western Union notification came in the dead of night. It was 1944 and Bobby was 12 years old.

"So they came to our door about 3:30 in the goddamn morning," Bobby said. "My mother was crying. You wake up and know something terrible has happened. My brother, Tommy was his name, was in the Naval Reserve. I didn't know him. I don't even remember him that much. He was on a transport plane in Idaho going from one base to another in terrible weather. The plane crashed. There were no survivors."

Losing a son was bad enough, but Bobby's parents left many relatives behind when they immigrated to the United States. Reading the story of the march of German Army boots and armor across Europe was especially painful for them.

"The one time I can remember seeing my father cry was when the Germans invaded Norway in 1940. I remember getting up for breakfast to go to school and, God it was so strange to see your father cry. I mean, Jesus I didn't know what the hell to do."

Bobby was closest to his brother Pete, a year older than Bobby, and his older sister Janie who told me, "My mother always said she had so little trouble with us four older ones. We weren't any trouble at all. She said when I got to Pete and Bobby, I got tired. She had six children in eight years. I can see where she'd get tired. But she was a sweet person."

To hear Pete tell it, "Bobby and I were just not part of the family. We didn't have the respect. The rest of the kids were respectful because they were closer to the parents. Bobby and I were sort of sittin' in the bleachers sayin' what's goin' on down there."

Pete – the dashing young kid and Bobby – the baby, had a long standing benevolent rivalry. "My brother Pete was the kinda guy in high school that was very much a member of the in-crowd," Bobby said. "Even though he was not athletic, he was a sharp dresser, a hip little high school kid. In my way of thinking, my brother was such a good looking guy and I was not a good looking guy and I'm sure that had a big effect on me when I was younger." Bobby always envied his brother and was self-conscious throughout his life about his own physical appearance, which could generously be described as not handsome. He was tall and walked with a shambling gait, wore thick rimmed glasses, had an affinity for books and music and loved high school. Bobby said, "I didn't do much work. I passed everything." Bobby and Pete even got a chance to raise hell together in the same class. Pete was flunking English and ended up in Bobby's class. "Yeah, I mean they held him over by popular demand," Bobby said. Held over for another six weeks. One day the teacher asked if I'd open the window a crack. It was winter time and I threw the window open and the next one. Pete was doin' the same thing. Finally, the teacher shouted, you Bastiensen's oughta be horsewhipped. She got right down to our fuckin' level."

Roosevelt High School was in what was considered a nice area of Minneapolis.

If you lived north of 35th street, that's where you went to school. Bobby and Pete lived in a neat two-story clapboard house on 33rd. So they were assigned to South High.

"South High had a far different clientele," Bobby said. "We saw a lot of blacks in school. I can only remember one or two that went to school when I did from grade school through junior high. But by the time I got to South High, I was really getting into jazz. And, of course that ultimately is gonna bring you to a lot of black musicians, man."

Bobby's older sister, Janie said, "It was a nice neighborhood. What I liked about it was you had many different ethnic people, a lot of blacks." For Bobby's father, a conservative immigrant from all white Norway, a quiet guy, it took some getting used to.

Bobby's father was a laborer at a foundry at Minneapolis Moline. "He was a sailor, a poor guy," Bobby recalled. "He was sailing on the ore boats and if you did that, you were off from December through April and you still got paid. Man, I mean it was the best of jobs."

But Bobby's mother ruled the roost. "My Dad was henpecked," Bobby said, "Mother did not want my Dad away from home. But he didn't know how to do anything, so he became a janitor. I remember when I was really little, going down into the basements of some of these big buildings where they had these huge furnaces, and you opened it with a hook. The fuckin' thing looked like hell, man."

"Bobby and I were just not part of the family."

While in school Bobby was averse to working. "Most guys had jobs part time or on weekends," Bobby said. "Not me. The thing I used to love was to go out and caddie. I loved golf courses even though I never played. Oh, I mean they were so gorgeous. I used to caddie at the Edina Country Club. And you know that big water tower in Edina? I won five dollars from a friend of mine. I bet him I'd have the nerve to go way up to the farthest crossbeam you could find and I just straddled it and inched my way across. Then, I climbed down and got my five dollars. That was a lot of money in those days."

Bobby, when he got older, worked on the ore boats for a while. "It's kind of hard to think of a job I didn't have," he said. He worked on The Rock Island Line, affixed tax stamps on the bottles of booze at the liquor warehouse, was a bottle spotter for Canada Dry making sure no foreign objects sullied the famous product, dove for golf balls at 4 in the morning at Edina Country Club, then sold them back to members outside the gate later in the day. "This was during the war, ya know and if you could get your hands on a Wilson K-28 or a Titleist, you could sell it for a little piece of money," Bobby said. Bobby also took a turn at polishing jelly beans and candy corn at the Powell Candy Company in Hopkins.

"The weirdest job was at The Jiffy Car Wash," Bobby said. "I walked in there in February of '53, the guy that owned it was white, the foreman was white and all the rest –

the ones who did the labor—were black."

As a teenager, Bobby was often at home alone, left to his own devices. Bobby said, "I was more a mother's boy, but only because I knew I could get away with a lot of stuff."

Street life opened a world of endless and exciting opportunity for trouble and Bobby had an infinite capacity for finding it.

In school, Bobby was always the class clown. As he tells it, "Yeah, I guess. Nobody could dress that way on purpose."

"Ya know, I was a real smart ass," he said. "I could bring people to the brink of destruction, ready to kill me with a gun or a knife, anything. A stake through the heart is what he needs."

Bobby's first teenage tragedy came in 9th grade at Falwell Junior High.

"So I'm in this woodworking class, and shop was as bad for me as anything was. I didn't know what was going on."

"It was me and another guy that were fuckin' around in class and the teacher was getting madder and madder."

The teacher, a man known for his uncontrollable temper and habit of grabbing students by the scruff of the neck and shaking them silly for not paying attention in class, was at his wits' end. And when Bobby presented his forlorn and unacceptable class project – a Rube Goldberg rendition of some unrecognizable invention – the teacher snapped.

"The weirdest job was at The Jiffy Car Wash."

Bobby said, "The guy went over like a fuckin' shot, man. Hit the fuckin' floor. That was a shocker. I mean, I hadn't ever seen a dead person, let alone caused them to fall over."

By age 14, Bobby Dale's reputation began to spread. One of his teachers called him a murderer. His friends, and he had many of those, thought he was cool and a natural born leader who could make them laugh.

It was a tough neighborhood. And a rough crowd at South High School made it dangerous.

Crime was a major pastime, especially if you were "a smart-assed mother's boy." While some teenagers played sandlot ball, Bobby and his football playing friend, Gordy Newstrom, "Go-Go" they called him, and a few others, were on a crime spree. And the local department stores, Dayton's, Donaldson's, Sears, and Nolander's, were the targets.

The plan was simple. Go-Go would create a diversion – knock a display off the counter and Bobby would make the grab. One day it was argyle socks, the next a stack of record albums. It was bold and they both knew they'd be caught sooner or later. But so what? What's the worst that could happen?

Bobby had a gift, a way of diverting your attention while he took care of business. Like that time he stole the transistor radio from Dayton's Department Store in downtown Minneapolis. He grabbed it off the shelf, turned on the Millers-Saints ballgame, put the radio to his ear and walked past the guard at the door who asked him the score. Another perfect crime. A daring daylight robbery and quite a rush for a teenager with no discernable skills.

They were in it for the thrills, the adrenalin rush was addictive and damn the consequences. They didn't even need, nor in some cases, even want the loot. "My mother would have spotted the stuff in a second," he said." It wasn't like the girls. Girls could always say, oh, I'm wearing Jeanie's sweater for a week." He stole because, "it was cheap thrills. It was fun," he said.

In eleventh grade, Bobby had his first serious brush with the law. He and a senior named Doug went on a covert clothes shopping spree at Donaldson's Department store. They loaded up on shirts, a sport coat and were divvying up the loot in the back seat of a friend's car parked behind Radio City Theatre when all hell broke loose.

Two police detectives, a man and a woman, ordered the boys out of the car. Bobby knew the woman from previous sightings on the street. And she knew him – had been on his case for five months. The man grabbed Bobby and Doug by their wrists and began dragging them down the alley behind the theater toward a waiting squad car. Doug – a stocky, Golden Glove Boxer who couldn't pronounce his r's yelled, "Wun, Babe," and punched the cop in the face, knocking him down, breaking his ankle. Bobby took off running.

Now Bobby was often chased by cops. But his boyhood friend, Jim Watkins recalls,

The youngest boys were essentially on their own.

"Poor Bobby was always left standing." Jim tells the story of the boys, "raisin' hell at a party at some girl's house. The cops were called and we ran, hitting the fence and scaling it, all except Babe. He was kinda lumbering. Not quite as agile as the rest. He said, 'I'll see ya Jimmy.' That's the last thing I remember as they grabbed him by the neck and hauled him off to jail."

Not this time. Bobby bolted eight blocks down Hennepin Avenue, before realizing that Doug didn't make it. But he was in the clear, for now. Bobby roamed the streets until early morning, fearing a trip home would get him busted. He slipped into bed at two in the morning, overslept and awoke with his mom at his bedside. "How could you," she said. And he knew. The cops were waiting downstairs.

He's not a bad boy.

2

"Glen Lake Home School for Boys."

Glen Lake Home School for Boys. Bobby was about to find out what happens to a 16-year-old boy after a petty crime spree. "The day that my little body was transported to Glen Lake, was the day that my brother, Pete, joined the Navy July 12, 1948."

Bobby said it was hard to forget, "with my mom collapsing on the bed every other minute – one boy leaving for boot camp, the other, for jail." His mother's sorrow was Bobby's delight. "Pete's goin' out the door and I'm kinda thrilled, 'cuz now I get all his fuckin' clothes."

Bobby was a clothes horse and older brother Pete, Bobby said, "dressed like Cary Grant. I keep a picture of my brother standing there with his Pepsodent smile and this beautiful sport jacket draped over his arm…and his tie. He's really a great looking, man." Bobby was a homely boy and it affected his self-esteem all his life. "When I used to walk into a class that my brother had been in the year before, it was a period of adjustment. You're Pete's brother. Jesus!"

But Pete's clothes would have to wait. At Glen Lake Bobby took psychological tests that he said determined, "I wasn't really what you call a bad boy." And what he got was a promise to get him back to South High for his

Bobby didn't have a mean bone in his body.

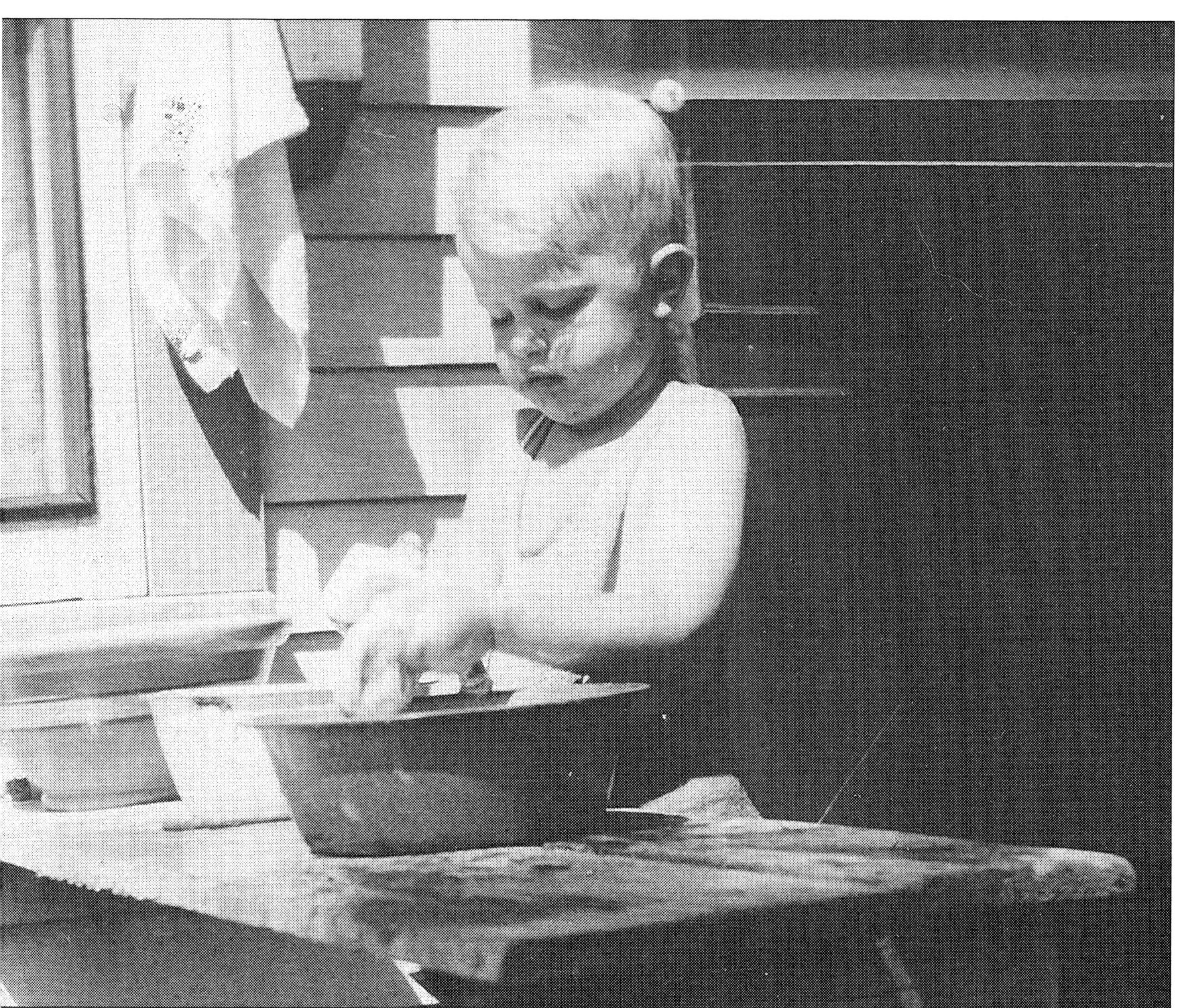

senior year in exchange for good behavior. Six weeks and he'd be off the hook.

Bobby toed the mark, but there wasn't all that much to do, "unless you were one of the lucky ones who worked on the farm," he said. "They raised their own food. They had their own milk. The only other kind of steady job was in the laundry, but nobody wanted to do that because you were in there for eight hours a day." Bobby didn't mind the job. At night, exhausted, he slept like a baby with about 300 other bunkmates in, "a huge dorm – a big room." The inmates ranged in age from 10 years to seventeen. Eighteen-year-olds went to Red Wing, the big house.

Bobby remembers the youngest of the young cons. "I mean he looked like a 10-year-old Frankenstein. Ya know, ten and eleven year olds in with guys like me. That's crazy. I mean to think somebody would be so bad to send him away at that age. It's fuckin' unreal. I don't think I even stole a yo-yo at that tender age."

Half the boys in the place were friends of Bobby. His reputation preceded him. Even after his release, Bobby would visit his pals – some serving long stretches that Bobby felt were unfair.

"This one friend – his name was George Keenan – really nice – the kinda guy that would never be in that kinda trouble. And the only thing this poor guy did was when we would steal a car – which was quite often – he would ride along. We would take a car on a Saturday night from a used car lot on Lake Street; usually we'd try to find a '30 Buick. You could work 'em without a key. And then we'd ride around in the car and take it back on Sunday night. Or else, abandon it on the street." And George Keenan got six months for his teenage miscalculation. "He was such a nice guy. You just want to protect him," Bobby said. Bobby always wanted to protect his friends.

"I wasn't really what you call a bad boy."

In the fall of 1948, Glen Lake kept its promise, releasing Bobby so that he could complete his senior year at South High. "I loved high school, man," he said. "I loved havin' a place to go and screw around." Bobby passed all his classes, but didn't do much work. He loved the screwin' around part most of all. He loved the football games and the bus trips to the away games in North Minneapolis. He was into music. He read the classics, poetry – anything he could get his hands on. He was voracious. But what he loved most was drinking beer and hanging out, the street life, joy riding in stolen cars, and occasional shoplifting to impress a girl.

Once he stole a cashmere sweater and gave it to a girl he'd been particularly fond of and admired secretly. "Oh Bobby," she said, "Thank you so much. Now I can go with Manny to the dance Saturday night." Bobby was not a ladies man. He was crushed.

The girls got pissed off that their boyfriends would rather spend time with Bobby than with them. Jim Watkins, his friend said,

Bobby seated on a hay bale, gets an early taste of life down on the farm.

"it was more fun at that early age if you could go out with Babe and the rest of the guys than maybe even going out dating with chicks, ya know?"

Jim and the others were attracted to Bobby's "great magnetism and charisma." Jim said, "he knew so goddamn much more than the rest of us. And the stories he'd tell." Bobby was, indeed, the leader of the pack – the Pied Piper. "He did a lot of good," Jim said. "He got a lot of kids following him and they did enjoy good music as well as kinda living on the fringes, so to speak. And they enjoyed good reading." Rubaiyat of Omar Khayyam by Edward Fitzgerald was on the reading list. Bobby memorized it. Poetry, for God's sake. What kind of a gang was this?

Pete in the Navy and Bobby, with his ever present cigarette.

3 Travelin' Light

"Thumbs went up and the adventure began."

It's hard to say when the Babe's wanderlust began. Maybe it was all those nights on the streets, catnaps in unlocked parked cars, and the thrill of carousing – anywhere the action was.

And on Saturday nights, the action was at the Pillsbury House, a hundred-year-old youth center where teenagers listened to music, danced, hung out.

February, 1951 – it was one of those Minnesota winters that forced you to thaw out your words in order to see what was being said. It was bone cold, and the Pillsbury House was packed.

Dallas Freeman, who was still a senior at South High, overheard Bobby saying that if he had $25 bucks, he'd be on his way to New Orleans. Teachers at South High were on strike at the time, Dallas was at loose ends and he told Bobby he had $75 dollars in his school savings plan that hadn't been touched since elementary school. Dallas said he'd loan Bobby the $25 – and off they went.

First they packed a couple of bags, got a few hours sleep. The next morning – February 8th Dallas recalls, it was his birthday – in 30-degree below zero weather they headed out, on foot, Lake street to Lyndale and out to Highway 65 South. Thumbs went up and the adventure began.

They made it as far as Kansas before Bobby and Dallas were forced to split up. There had been a horrific murder, people were paranoid and nobody would be picking up a pair of hitchhikers in that neck of the woods. They hooked up farther on down the road.

They made it to New Orleans. They spent a couple of nights with two guys from Brazil who were in the States studying coffee handling – whatever that is. The next two nights were spent in the bus depot and the rest of the time in bars. "They never close, you know," Dallas said.

"We were underage, but they had no problem serving us," he said. The locals bought them drinks and showered them with hospitality for having hitchhiked all that way from the upper end of the Mississippi to celebrate with them along the Delta.

"They even bought us food," Dallas said. "Now isn't that something? You can get by with murder when you're young. We had a really good time."

Bobby made the trip to the Mardi Gras from 1950 through 1955. He missed 1953 when his brother got married and, as Bobby put it, "I hadda stay for the wedding. I was not too happy. I really wasn't."

"Half naked people were running around drinking."

Bobby said it would have been fun to try the New Orleans adventure with money. But that didn't happen and each trip was an exercise in creativity. He said, "You learn how to spin a story. Some of these guys I got a ride with wouldn't tell you how far they were going. They wanted to see how compatible you'd be. And every ride you ever got, believe me, you paid for by listening to some of the most fuckin' boring stories imaginable. My wife doesn't understand me. I'm a switch hitter."

Rejecting unwanted advances became an art in itself, and Bobby would spend many nights at the local bus station. "Either that or jails," he said. "In the smaller cities and towns you could just go to the local jail and offer to sweep it out in the morning, and they'd say great. Come in. Have coffee and donuts. It was great." Bobby of course knew his way around jails, having spent more nights than he could count sleeping off a beer night at a local jazz club.

The weekend before Mardi Gras in 1950, Bobby woke up on the couch in some strangers' apartment, saw his friend Dallas was in the bed, and he could hear the noise. He said, "The apartment was right on Bourbon Street and it was the first time that I actually saw Mardi Gras during the day. It was nine in the morning. I slipped out for a look and you couldn't fuckin' believe it, you know? Half-naked people were running around drinking. I ran upstairs. I got fuckin' Dallas up. And away we went down Bourbon Street. And you know you didn't need any money. You just needed a glass. And we slept in Jackson Square during the day. It's such a fabulous city to wander around in." Bobby was addicted to New Orleans.

It was the music that cast the spell over Bobby. "One year, I remember seeing the name, Clarence Frogman Henry on a marquee at some club on Bourbon Street. He was the guy who had, *Ain't Got No Home.* Chris Kenner, *I Like it Like That...* all those cats were from around there, and, of course, Dr. John."

He didn't know it at the time, but Bobby's love of jazz and rhythm and blues would serve him well after his most serious brush with the law that would change his life forever.

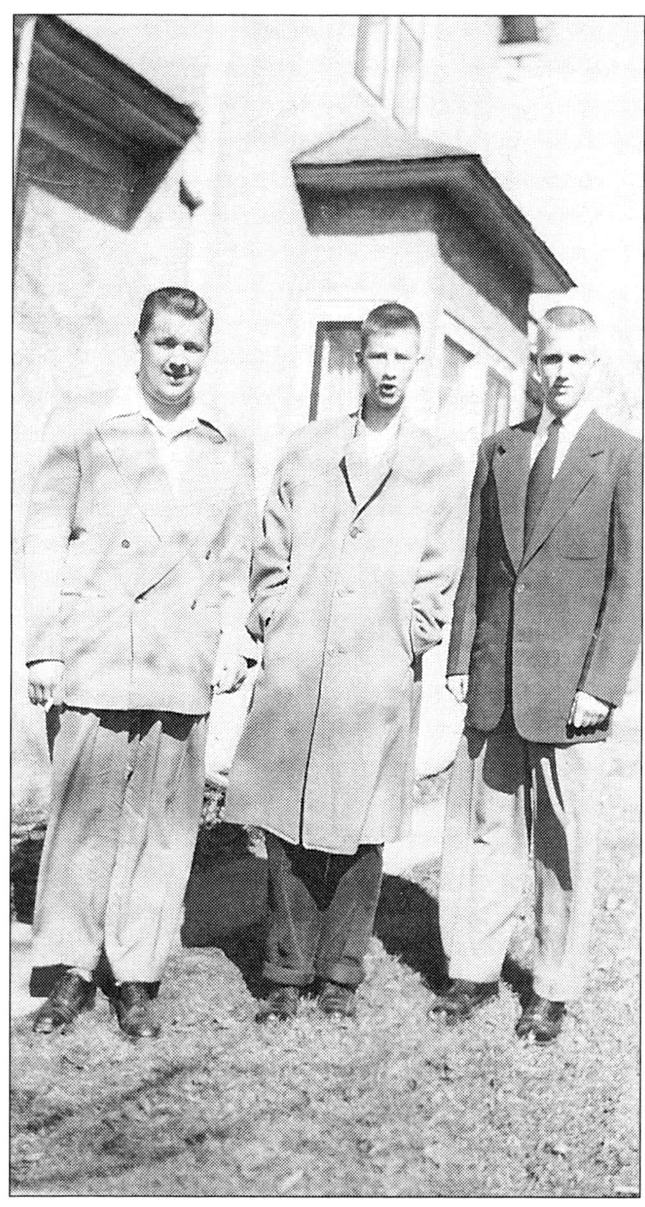

Bobby stands between friends for a reluctant pose.

4 Manslaughter

"Bobby always enjoyed a good tenor sax."

It was February – 30 below zero. Steam rose from street grates. And there were patches of slippery black ice on the pavement.

Just back from his first trip to New Orleans, where revelers ran half naked by day, Bobby and a couple pals were braced in heavy coats against the brittle wind after leaving the Cassius Jazz Club at closing time. The Cassius was a neighborhood joint catering to a mostly black crowd with Chinese apartments above, Chinese writing on the outside, and the bar on the first floor.

Irv Williams had been the headliner that night – a tenor sax man Bobby dug who'd been with Count Basie before settling in the Twin Cities. Irv had run into Bobby and the other kids when playing for the Saturday night dances at The Pillsbury House. Bobby always enjoyed a good tenor sax and he loved the way Irv Williams played *Stardust.*

It was a Saturday night and as Bobby recalls, "maybe I had one beer, if that. They must have known we weren't 21. But since we were the type that never caused trouble in there…ya know? It was a nice little club." The trouble started when they were leaving the club. So much trouble, it made the front page of the Minneapolis Star and Tribune.

Here's how Bobby tells it: "We went from the club to Cedar and Lake, to a place called Emily and Frenchies – a hamburger joint we hung out at. It was closed. So we're walkin' down Lake from Cedar to Bloomington. There were a couple of hamburger joints down there where we could get something to eat. When we got to 18th Street and Lake, this guy starts honking his fuckin' horn as we're crossing the street. And he says, get the fuck out of the way.'"

Bobby was walking with a couple of friends: Joe Halpin, described by some who knew him as a wild and crazy guy, and Gordy Newstrom, the tough guy they called "Go-Go," who worked with Bobby on his shoplifting sprees.

After the exchange of words at the intersection, "this huge dude," Bobby called him, "starts getting out of the car. Joe slammed the door on the guy, he goes down and Joe kicked him in the head. And then this even bigger guy got out and we took off down the street."

The big guy caught up, and on the corner of 17th and Lake, he got into it with Go-Go.

It was a wrestling match with short punches delivered for effect. The big guy says he's an off duty cop. Go-Go, who has him pinned to the ground said they didn't want any trouble, "if I let you up, will you let us get the hell out of here?"

The cop said sure, but when Go-Go loosened his grip, the violent dance continued through the plate glass window of Nolanders Department Store. The cop was cut. The boys – all on probation – scattered. And, once again, Bobby went into hiding. "I knew this was not gonna be good," he said. "I went home really late and I went upstairs to my room. Then I slipped into my sister's room which faced the street. And there, I could see the spotlight looking for the address. So I just got my fuckin' clothes on, went downstairs, met the cops at the door, told my mother it had nothing to do with me. I'm a witness." And off he went to jail ...again. This time it was serious. The broken store window had severed the femoral artery of the off duty cop. He bled to death.

"I spent the rest of the night talking with other inmates on the 5th floor of the Minneapolis Courthouse," Bobby recalls. "One guy was facing 40 years in Stillwater and he's got his arm around my shoulder – comforting me. All of a sudden, something was thrown at the bars of the cell."

There were two cops outside the cell – brothers of the officer who had died. They had the look of men who wanted a piece of Bobby Dale. The dead cop, had had five or six kids in fact, and three brothers who were police officers, as Bobby recalled.

As it turned out, he and his partner had been sitting in the Bee Hive Tavern since two o'clock that afternoon with a bottle of bourbon and beer chasers.

They were dead drunk when they tangled with the boys on Lake Street. There also were 30 witnesses to the confrontation and the Grand Jury returned a no bill. The boys were free to roam. But it would never be the same.

5 The Open Door

"30 days at Parker Lake."

The drunken brawl on Lake Street was serendipity. Four guys who knew each other, but hadn't seen or been with each other in ages, met on that corner. The hamburger joint was closed and a cop died. Bobby said, "It was like some weird movie. It was bizarre, the whole thing." And it changed Bobby's life.

There were ripple effects. A subpoena was served at the Jiffy Car Wash three years later ordering Bobby to appear in court after the family of the dead cop sued the Cassius Jazz Club for serving liquor to underage drinkers. And the police kept on Bobby's case. He was placed in a lineup, "just to humiliate me," Bobby said. "The guy would look at me and say, now this guy is Bobby. His name is Robert Dale Bastiensen and although he's been in trouble with the law many times, you know one thing for sure, it's never his fault. He just always happens to be there."

The cops also wanted Bobby to go up and down Lake Street and see how many bars would serve him. They would sit outside in their squad car. Bobby was to signal them and the 3/2 beer joint was busted. It happened just once. But that was one time too many.

"One time, Bobby said, "I was waiting for a friend to come home, and I'm sitting on his step sleeping. And the next thing you know

Bobby said his brother Pete "dressed like Cary Grant."

I'm in a paddy wagon and the cops are talking and one says, we got the stocking cap bandit. That's who you are. And I'm back in court again. The judge was Neddy Washburn and she said, 'I've had it. I've seen too much of you.' It was like watching Judge Judy. So it was 30 days at Parker Lake - the work house, ya know?- for being drunk in public."

By this time, Bobby said his folks were so horrified over everything that happened, they moved to Excelsior, a small town west of Minneapolis where Bobby was never arrested. But then he was hardly ever there.

Life went on in South Minneapolis where Bobby stayed with friends or slept in unlocked parked cars; he was beginning to get his fill of cops, robbers and jail time. He was locked up six or seven times. In those days, if you were drunk on the street, you could be held incognito for up to 72 hours. And Bobby received that treatment, twice. Once was during the great blizzard of '51. Minneapolis was wiped out, but Bobby didn't see a single snowflake from his six by eight jail cell.

Bobby seldom, if ever, went to his folks' new home in Excelsior. It was too far away and Bobby had no car. "In order to get a car, Bobby said, you'd have to go to work. I never let that interfere with listening to music and drinking. I had an image to uphold."

That was all about to change, in a big way.

6 The Way Out

"He was 20. She was 16."

Bobby had just gotten off probation when he met his first and only real girlfriend at a party. Carol Johnson, a Norwegian girl. He was 20. She was 16.

Carol said, "I dated plenty but there was never anyone like Bobby. He was cynical and funny, had a great sense of music and, yes he was bald, but he appealed to me." Bobby still had no confidence with women, "but I got along with them great," he said. "They told me stuff that they wouldn't tell anybody but their girlfriends. I was a fun guy to be around and didn't have the nerve to ask them if they'd like to indulge…in whatever."

At the party there was the usual beer and laughter. Bobby and Carol, his new young admirer, would hook elbows "like the Germans do and drink that way and laugh about it," Carol recalled. They talked and later in the evening Bobby did what he does best – he easily became the life of the party.

Bobby always was self-conscious about appearing before crowds, but with his small circle of devoted friends and an ample supply of beer, he became riotously funny. He could pick up a movie magazine or newspaper and spontaneously twist a tabloid tale into an absurd social commentary. He was genius at the art of ad lib. And because of his bookish ways, complimented with a photographic memory, he created a patter that was music to the ears of his "gang." He had a great knowledge of jazz which drew many people to him. That was the thing in those days. Gangs aren't what they used to be.

As Carol tells it, "Bobby got into one of his monologues that were all creative and he'd just have everybody just laughing like crazy, then he just went off into the bedroom and fell asleep. I used to wonder why when he had everybody just so enjoying themselves and him, the center of it, would he just disappear. He did that quite often in those days."

It was like watching a light bulb burning brightly and then suddenly fading to black. It was the pattern of his life. He loved center stage, his adoring fans, and the laughter. But when the alcohol burned off Bobby always withdrew into his private world of music and books.

College life at the University of Minnesota was short but sweet: music appreciation, history, humanities and speech. Three A's and a D. The D was in speaking. "I went there about a year-and-a-half," Bobby recalled. "Of course I kept dropping out to hitchhike to New Orleans for Mardi Gras. I mean, we have to take care of our social obligations."

Returning from one of those trips in 1955, his traveling companion, Jack Latsall, said he was going to check out The Brown Institute of the Air, a radio school on Lake Street, not far from Bobby's home. "It's really hard to explain," Bobby said. "When I walked in there they had me read a little something. I think they would have taken you if you'd been Harpo Marx, but I'm tellin' you man." Bobby was hooked.

Much later in his career when asked by fellow San Francisco disc jockey, Bobby Mitchell, how he'd gotten into radio, Bobby replied, "It wasn't how I got in. It was that I was too old for hitchhiking, so I had to find something." His new girlfriend, Carol, encouraged him to sign up, loaned him the money, and the Babe began the adventure of his life. "For the first time in my life I had something I was excited about except getting drunk or stealing. Because it was fun, man and something I could do well."

Twenty-seven weeks of fun being taught the tricks of the trade by Howard Viken who owned the mornings on WCCO radio – Bobby's first teacher. Irv Smith – The Tune Smith – was Bobby's favorite teacher. "He was a fuckin' gas. He invited us to watch him work at WDGY before it became a top Storz Station. So we went and watched him being an announcer. And it was incredible, man. That was for me."

Bobby couldn't wait to get to school every night. He was top student in his class for twenty-seven weeks. In the end students were promised a job. No guarantee the job would be in Minneapolis, a major market, but Bobby wasn't fussy and it's a good thing.

7 The Way West

"Glendive, Montana...Stan Getz and Chet Baker."

Bobby chose Glendive, Montana to begin his radio career at KXGN-AM, a random pick from the map on the wall at radio school. Glendive was looking for someone immediately. Bobby made an audition tape, sent it out and was hired within days. Students were encouraged not to wait around for jobs in Minneapolis because it would be a long wait. "Where you start is not important," they said.

Carol Johnson not only helped Bobby pay for radio school but loaned him money for a car, a 1950 Plymouth, that he loaded up with books and albums and pointed toward Big Sky country in early January, 1956.

Bobby pulled into Glendive in eastern Montana just before dawn on Friday the 13th, drove to the radio station and was asked if he wanted to report the 6am news. And Bobby Dale, dead tired after his 600-mile drive, began his radio career in earnest.

The following Monday, Bobby pulled his regular shift – noon until 6pm The noon hour was all news. At 1pm: organ music and a "Daily Thought" from the general manager. At two, a one-hour disc jockey show. "So what am I playin?" asks Bobby, "Stan Getz and Chet Baker."

Glendive in 1956 was a farm, fishing, and wildlife community with a population around 25,000 people, half of them highly paid young men – many of them engineers - managing the oil fields discovered in Glendive in 1952. The Yellowstone River, where the Lewis and Clark Expedition camped out in 1806, runs through the middle of town.

Fishing was great, star gazing was spectacular, but since there was no television reception, a good time consisted of a visit to the town's whorehouse, Twenty Acres Ranch, or listening to the radio and hanging out in the bar at the Hill Hotel. That's where all the oil guys stayed and where they drank and where they gave Bobby an earful every night about his radio program. They listened while driving the oil fields and when Bobby asked them what they wanted to hear, it was always something off the top 40.

By 1956 "Rock 'n Roll" was in full swing. Elvis Presley was quickly ascending toward his throne. He made his national television debut in January. His first major hit for RCA records –*Heartbreak Hotel*– was released a month later and jumped to number one. Carl Perkins' *Blue Suede Shoes* strolled to number two. In fact, Elvis had five number one hits in 1956. There was an explosion of popular music and radio stations everywhere reaped the rewards. Their listeners couldn't get enough of it. And it was an eye opener for Bobby.

"It was always *Green Door* by Jim Lowe, so I started playin' popular music. And the oil boys loved it, man. You know, they had their own request line going. They would return the favor and buy me drinks."

Bobby had no money. He earned $45 dollars a week. Fifteen of that went for rent each month in the basement of a nearby house, and the rest went to Carol Johnson to pay off his car loan.

Carol's "Dear John" letter arrived in Glendive that summer. When Bobby went home on vacation in the fall, he attended a high school football game at South High and that night was having a drink at a bar. "They had a guy playing a piano, and who walks in but Carol and her girlfriend, Nancy." Bobby hadn't responded to Carol's letter telling him it was over between them. But the next morning, Bobby did muster the courage to drive to Carol's house. "She wouldn't see me again, Bobby said. So I just pissed around Minneapolis for a little bit and drove back to Glendive."

But Glendive was about to become a memory, a fond memory for Bobby who'd often mention Glendive and the Montana prairie in his adlibs about the early days. Now it was time to get closer to home, to Carol, and, maybe, it would all work out. By December, 1956 he took the first step back and landed in Fargo, North Dakota.

8 At the Hop

"KFGO radio had a big reach."

Fargo was not a big market but KFGO radio had a big reach – 5,000 watts that stretched into Canada. And unlike pleasing the "oil boys" at the Hill Hotel in Glendive, now there were packs of energized teenagers who needed to shoo-bop shoo-bop. Bobby Dale was their six-to-midnight weekday platter spinner. On the weekends he was their reluctant, self conscious host at the hop.

A simple concept: your favorite DJ with a stack of Top 40 records under his arm, a turntable, a couple of speakers and you've got a party. They called them platter parties, sock hops (leave your shoes at the door and don't scuff the gymnasium floor) but mostly they were simply record hops. And Bobby hated them. They were an important part of the top 40 game, and it meant extra money in your pocket. But it meant getting up in front of a crowd, an unruly crowd at that. And for Bobby that was pure hell. "Well, ya know they say you get over things…like your self consciousness," he said. "But I never did."

Bobby's closest friend in Fargo was Charlie Boone, a preacher's kid who began his radio career in Wadena, Minnesota. Charlie had one of those classic radio voices, a love of Frank Sinatra music and a certain unease about the budding phenomenon known as Top 40 radio.

Top 40 became a way of life.

But since the program director left Fargo shortly after Charlie was hired, Charlie became the program director, inheriting Bobby Dale and a mandate to produce a number one rated radio station.

Fargo is a small market surrounded by prairie and the "mighty 790" reached not only into Canada but climbed every hill and dale in eastern North and South Dakota and western Minnesota, including nearby Moorhead, Minnesota. It was a perfect training ground for a preacher's son and a self conscious, funny street kid named Bobby Dale whom Charlie soon discovered was his ace in the hole. Bobby had a sixth sense about popular music. He didn't like all of it, but somehow he knew what music would become a hit. "He was uncanny in his ability to recognize hits," Charlie recalled. "He was one of the most talented disc jockey's I've ever known."

So Charlie left the music to Bobby. Charlie managed the staff and the record hops, taking the pressure off Bobby whom Charlie knew had big issues about making personal appearances. "He was conscious about his appearance," Charlie said. "He was a big guy, losing his hair. He was not the most attractive person visually. And I think he was quite sensitive about that. People visualized him in a different way and when they saw him, they were probably disappointed to be honest. The reaction was, gee I didn't think he'd look like that. Bobby was very conscious of the fact he couldn't get the woman he wanted and I'm sure he attributed it to the fact that he wasn't as handsome as he wanted to be."

It was a struggle for Bobby all his life. And now with Carol's Dear John letter on his dresser, Bobby became more troubled than ever. According to his new friend Charlie Boone, "he drank to excess to forget, I think. He liked to sing the blues, and loved to listen to maudlin blues and just pine for his girlfriend. He was a lonely guy, and a sweet and talented guy."

Charlie took on the job of protecting Bobby. "We saved his ass so many times because he liked to drink. I used to get frustrated with him because he would screw up. But you would forgive him immediately. He was a forgivable person."

Charlie worked noon to 6pm Bobby from 6pm 'til midnight. On the weekends Bobby and Charlie would climb in Charlie's Karmen Ghia and head for the Saturday night platter party in some small town. "It was really something," Bobby recalled. "We got free advertising for the hops, and maybe 150-dollars cash for the night. Before I knew it I was driving around in a nice car with a cashmere sportcoat which I promptly burned with a cigarette…just to prove it was mine."

Then came the day in June of 1957 when Bobby's rock 'n roll radio show literally was blown apart.

9

Whole Lotta Shakin' Goin' On

"A good bar was home to Bobby."

Bobby's show began like always, at six pm At 6:10 the little red bulb on the studio phone began blinking nervously. It was the airport weather line, used to supply area radio stations with the latest temperature, humidity and wind readings for the Fargo area. Only this time it was a tornado warning – a "monstrous" tornado in the area that meant take cover.

"So I gave the little warning and said what people should do if the worst happened – and it did," Bobby said. "Now we're talkin' to the weather guy and I'm doin' a records show. Every record I was playing caused me paranoia. *Whole Lotta Shakin' Goin' On, So Rare*...anything man. Finally, I couldn't play any more records and just talked...and the phone rang again and the guy wanted to know where the station was located. I said we're maybe one block off Broadway on Northern Avenue – right in downtown Fargo. The guy says, "Jesus, get the hell out of there. It's comin' man."

Bobby panicked, ran down the stairs and into the street covered by nothing but blue sky. "It looked like an ad for Hawaii, man," Bobby recalled. "I'm not kidding. Then I walked to the corner which was only about ten feet from where I was standing."

And there it was, big and ominously black. It was one of the biggest twisters

1957- Fargo Tornado leaves unimaginable devastation.

in America over 50 years of keeping records. It ripped up 22 blocks and killed more than 10 people.

Bobby then discovered that his station was the only radio station still on the air. All the others had been knocked out by the storm leaving Bobby Dale with the job of informing the community of emergency services at the Minnesota Moorhead Armory and the activities of the National Guard that had been called out.

"I knew it was really bad," Bobby said. "I had no idea that tornadoes were so weird – that if you looked one way you didn't see anything, until you peeked around the corner. The thing finally blew itself out on the golf course."

Charlie Boone, Bobby's friend and fellow jock had been at home listening to Bobby's tornado coverage: "He's the only guy on the radio who could make a tornado sound funny. I'm lookin' out the window. I'm livin' in

Moorhead. I'm out the door and rooftops are flyin' over my head. I knew this was pretty bad. I'm seein' flyin' shingles and Bobby…he's funny. He got serious, of course, when it was necessary to get serious. He wasn't irresponsible. But he had the ability to put a funny twist on a twister."

Radio had indeed saved Bobby's life. "I'm sure that's true, Charlie said. "He finally found an outlet – a healthy outlet for his humor and he loved to play the hits and he loved to pick'em."

Bobby always had a golden ear for lyrics. "Oh yeah," Bobby said. "I was really a fan of the Cole Porters and people like that. The first year in probably one of the first Billboard Magazines I ever read in 1956, I'm looking at their 100 best selling records in the country. And at 60 something was *In the Still of the Night* by The Five Satins. And I thought, my god man, they're doin' Cole Porter. This is fantastic. I must get this record. Of course when I heard *In the Still of the Night*, I fell in love with it. Just an incredible record. Of course, it didn't have much to do with Cole Porter. But it would make a good trivia question: What Cole Porter song was the last song of his to go top ten? Can you tell me? I'll tell you who sang it: Grace Kelly and Bing Crosby; *True Love* (singing) I give to you and you give to me…true love. Yeah it was in the top ten."

Charlie began to realize that Bobby Dale was someone special. "I never really had arguments with Charlie about music," Bobby said. "But, he used to crack me up 'cuz he used to say: 'I don't give a damn man…if you're telling me that we can't play one Sinatra record, that it's gonna kill us here?' Then the next thing I hear is *Come Fly with Me*.

"I'm seein' flying shingles and Bobby...he's funny."

"He was much more complex than we all realized," Charlie recalled, "and much more intellectual. He was very, very sensitive. I think of Bobby as the most unforgetable character I've ever met in radio. And I've met a lot of them."

Charlie did get his fill of Frank Sinatra in the wee hours. Bobby would get off at midnight and head for the FM Hotel in Moorhead, across the state line. North Dakota's last call was midnight. It took Bobby awhile to realize the bars in Minnesota were open until one in the morning. But once he did, he was a regular. A good bar was home to Bobby.

Charlie would often join Bobby for drinks. "Bobby'd be in his cups, Charlie said. He'd have a couple of scotches. He loved scotch. And I remember going over to his pad and just playing music – one album after another of Sinatra. *Only the Lonely* was one I remember very well:

"If you find love hang on to each caress. And never let it go. For when it's gone you'll know the loneliness. The heartbreak only the lonely know."

Bobby still had it bad for Carol – the girl back home who weighed heavily on his heart. By morning, the cloud had lifted but Carol was still on his mind. And Bobby had to see her. It wasn't pretty.

10 To Know Him Is To Love Him

Bobby's first hit record, the first of many.

"They threw my ass in jail."

Bobby headed for Minneapolis. "It was on a Saturday night," Bobby said. "Carol was babysitting with a friend. The minute I walked in the door, I knew something was up. And guess what was playing? She was playing an album I'd given her by Billie Holiday with this great song, *You've Changed. You're not the Angel I Once Knew.* Carol just said 'I'm sorry I just don't want to go out anymore.' And I left."

Bobby called Bob Serempa, a record promoter and co-owner of a one-stop record distribution operation out of Minneapolis. Bobby said he was in town. Serempa said c'mon over, we're havin' a wild party. "So I went over to Serempa's," Bobby said, "and got totally shit-faced. And then Sunday night I did the same thing and that's when I got arrested for drunk driving. They threw my ass in jail. The next day you're allowed one phone call. I called Serempa for the hundred dollar bail money."

Serempa got the money from his partner who had no use for disc jockeys and demanded Bobby remain in the office until he was repaid with a money order from good old Charlie Boone.

"I had such a hangover," Bobby recalled. "I'd been drinking wine by the gallon...dying of thirst. And I'm laying on the couch in Serempa's office, ya know? Just sick.

Doré
45 RPM
45 RPM
TO KNOW HIM, IS TO LOVE HIM
THE TEDDY BEARS
45-503

And suddenly I hear this record that I just started playing in Fargo. It was called *To Know Him Is To Love Him* by the Teddy Bears. And one of the Teddy Bears, of course, was Phil Spector. I didn't even know who Phil Spector was. In fact, I didn't know even after Phil and I became good friends that he was one of the singers. I didn't like the record, but I sure thought it was a hit."

The Dore label mailed out the record to radio stations in the fall of 1958. The A-side, the side being promoted, was a song called, *You Don't Know My Little Pet.* Bobby flipped it over, played *To Know Him Is To Love Him* and unwittingly launched the career of Phil Spector.

"The first time I played that record, the phones lit up – kids callin' about it, ya know? So man, I pulled myself off that couch and said to Serempa, is that your record? He said yeah, why? I said because it's gonna be a...if not number one...at least top ten in the country. He said, you're kiddin', Bobby. That's a piece of shit. I said ya know I'm not 18 anymore or 16, but believe me I'm already playing it. You get Bill Stewart, who was programming the Storz radio stations, tell him you're not going to like this record but this is a fuckin' monster, and Serempa did that. He got it on WDGY in Minneapolis, then in Kansas City, Miami. All you had to do was play it and it was over, man. And that was how that whole thing happened, man."

"I didn't like the record, but I sure thought it was a hit."

The Dore label received an order for 18,000 copies of the record and Phil Spector reportedly thought it was a misprint or a joke of some kind. Spector called to confirm and Serempa increased his order. Soon after, radio stations across the country jumped on the record, the Teddy Bears appeared on American Bandstand and the record shot to number one, selling over a million copies. It would not be the last national hit Bobby Dale would get credit for.

Bobby got his bail money from Charlie, paid Serempa back and nursed a bad hangover on the train ride back to Fargo. It wasn't long before Bobby's reputation paved his way to greater success. He was about to do battle with the big boys at Storz Broadcasting – one of the big guns in the Top 40 wars.

To Know Him Is To Love Him

Words and Music by PHIL SPECTOR

Recorded on Dore Records by THE TEDDY BEARS Recorded on Roulette Records by CATHY CARR Recorded on Capitol Records by EVELYN KINGSLEY with THE TOW

PRICE
50c
(In U. S. A.)

WARMAN MUSIC CO.

Sole Selling Agents

CRITERION MUSIC CORP.

1270 6th Ave. Radio City, N. Y.

Bobby would become known as "The Golden Ear."

11

The Golden Age of Rock'n Roll

"Bobby's misspent youth was now paying off."

Al Jarvis was called America's first real disc jockey. In 1934 when radio shows helped create the images in our head, Al Jarvis was creating radio history in Los Angeles. He brought images of dancers, musicians and ballroom wallflowers to life in his "Make Believe Ballroom", playing the music of Benny Goodman, Lionel Hampton, Nat King Cole and other big names who had Jarvis to thank for launching their careers. And it was Al Jarvis who started the first teenage dance show on television in Los Angeles. He was a true pioneer who didn't get all the credit he deserved.

Most radio and music historians give Alan Freed "first" disc jockey credits for kicking off the new generation of music for teenagers on his radio program.

Freed began playing all rhythm and blues records for a white teenage audience July 11th, 1951 on WJW radio in Cleveland. The R&B, as it was called, was performed primarily by black musicians, and to temper racial prejudices so prevalent at the time, Freed called it something else – rock 'n roll. The irony is that the term was black slang for sex, creating storms of protest among parents and members of the white establishment who regarded this new music, rebellious, sexual and anti-social. The fear and loathing surrounding rock 'n roll was palpable, Time magazine called it "vulgar," "new lows in taste." A columnist for the New York World Telegram said rock 'n roll was "contrived by corrupt men."

But white middle class teenagers were hooked on it. Freed named his program "Moondog's Rock 'n Roll Party" and became the most famous disc jockey in rock 'n roll history.

The phenomenon spread like prairie fire. Disc jockeys like Waxie Maxie in Washington D.C., Hunter Hancock in L.A., and Porky Chedwick in Pittsburgh began following Freed's lead and by 1953 rock 'n roll was here to stay coast to coast.

Within months Freed was putting on shows and in March of 1952, at his Moondog Coronation Ball in Cleveland, 25,000 mostly white fans showed up. It was a near riot. By 1954 Freed had taken his franchise to WINS in New York where he became legendary for not only his radio talent, but for refusing to play "white covers" – what major record companies considered acceptable white versions of songs originally recorded by black artists. Pat Boone was most notable among white cover artists. Boone was a "crooner," but for his debut on the Dot record label, he released *Two Hearts, Two Kisses* – covering the Otis Williams and the Charms original. Boone's cover was not a huge success but the die had been cast. Boone's follow up was pure gold, covering Fats Domino's *Ain't That a Shame.* It was number one for weeks in 1955 and inspired the further softening of black music. Boone "whitened" The Flamingo's *I'll Be Home* and Little Richard's *Tutti Frutti* and *Long Tall Sally.* Alan Freed would have none of it. He called Boone's records "watered down steals from the new Bing Crosby," and refused to play them. The "covers" were the records promoted by the record companies and disc jockeys and Freed's refusal to play them created enemies.

Down in Memphis, a less well known disc jockey named Dewey Phillips was making headlines playing black rhythm and blues, white country music, boogie-woogie and jazz for a mixed race audience. There were, in fact, radio experiments underway in all regions of the country, each unique in their own way.

In the south, R&B music was banned on several radio stations. It was called "race music" and strongly opposed by prejudiced southerners soon to become embroiled in the tumult and tragedy of the civil rights struggle.

It was the age of desegregation, white teenagers in the south embraced rock 'n roll and blues instead of country music. Country artists like Elvis Presley, Conway Twitty, Carl Perkins, Jerry Lee Lewis and the Everly Brothers crossed over and gave us *Heartbreak Hotel, Whole Lotta Shakin' Goin' On, Blue Suede Shoes,* and *Jailhouse Rock* – a fusion of country and blues that captured the imagination of young people everywhere.

Bobby Dale's own experience in Montana, young people clamoring for more traditional country music, began shaping the future of what would soon become the rock 'n roll explosion. A bonus for Bobby, of course, was his encyclopedic knowledge of musical history and a vast library of albums acquired diligently in a crime spree not seen before or since. "I was such a music snob," Bobby said. "If anybody brought blues records or any of that shit around me when I was a teenager, I, of course, knew everything there was to know about music. And I, of course, used to carry my albums with the pictures showing – Miles and Charlie Parker together and things of that nature…to improve my image." Bobby's misspent youth was now paying off.

In his book, *The Hits Just Keep on Coming*, author Ben Fong-Torres wrote, "Bobby had a jazz soul, a love of music ranging from pop to blues, folk and jazz." That he did, and over the next four decades he would influence our changing musical culture in significant ways.

Rock 'n roll music took hold of an enormous younger generation captivated by the rhythm, the backbeat and the energy of it. It was a teenage invention, and Bobby Dale, still in his early 20's like all young disc jockeys, got caught up in the excitement as well.

Todd Storz got Rock Radio rolling at about the same time at KOWH-AM in Omaha, Nebraska. Popular legend has it that Storz, the station manager and Bill Stewart, his program director – after observing customers at a tavern in Omaha dropping nickels into the juke box, playing their favorite songs over and over – gave birth to Top 40 radio. It's a nice story, but it didn't happen that way.

Storz was programming sponsored programs, variety shows and radio dramas, and every so often he squeezed in some popular music. His listeners couldn't get enough of it and were flocking to record stores and playing their favorites repeatedly on the jukebox first introduced in 1951.

Storz bought more radio stations: WTIX-AM in New Orleans and in 1954, WHB-AM, a powerhouse station in Kansas City, Missouri.

WHB could be heard throughout the Midwest and Great Plains. Storz made it an "all hits" radio station and called it "Top 40." WHB broadcast the first Top 40 countdown

Gordon McClendon – the legendary Texas broadcaster paid close attention to what Storz was doing, copied and perfected it and soon Top 40 stations were popping up all over the country. Rock 'n roll roots were spreading wide and deep. And Bobby Dale was in the thick of it.

Bobby moved to KOIL-AM in Omaha in December of 1958. His record distributor friend, Bob Serempa had a hand in his getting the job. And even though Omaha was not a big market, Bobby felt the buzz when he arrived. "I'm wondering why all these people were treating me like I was really somebody," Bobby said. "But I forgot that Omaha was a market that Todd Storz operated out of." Bobby was there to compete against Storz. And it was in Omaha where Bobby's real radio education began.

Don Burdon was a young promotion guy who bought KOIL-AM for $185,000 dollars with a $5,000 dollar down payment in 1952 – all the money he had. In January of 1953, the intense competition with Todd Storz's KOWH began. Burdon had the advantage from the start. KOIL was a 24-hour-a-day operation. KOWH – the Storz station – was a daytimer – meaning it had to shutdown at midnight. Burdon also stole some of Storz's top name talent. The legendary Gary Owens and Don Steele came out of KOIL.

Todd Storz fought back, getting Gary Owens hired away from KOIL by KIMN in Denver. Bobby was hired to do nights. "I thought I was gonna be doin' like I was in Fargo," Bobby said. "I really liked that; just playin' rock 'n roll records and a few commercials. That was it. It was great." But what Bobby got was the drive time morning show of Denver bound Gary Owens – 5:25 until 9:00am – weird hours for a man who loved bar

"I'm thinking, Jesus this guy is killing me."

closings. "My favorite bar, The Red Lion, burned down in Omaha…on a Saturday morning," Bobby recalled. "This is where I hung out, and lived there practically." When Bill Stewart, the programming guy for all the Storz stations, was fired, he ended up at KOIL as the program director and every afternoon was down at the Red Lion with Bobby Dale. "We'd go to the hotel bar and there we'd sit and drink…which was great," Bobby said. "He did all the buying. I didn't have the money for it. We'd be out at night and he'd say 'now listen I'm gonna set my alarm for 5:20 tomorrow morning and I'll wake and you better fuckin' be there pal. You shouldn't be drunk. We love ya. Be there at 5:25,' and I'm thinking, Jesus, this guy's killin' me."

And then Bobby told his saddest Omaha story: "One morning when I came to work…on a Saturday... and I'm reading the local news for Omaha. I'm reading it without looking, of course, like you always rip and read. And I read: On the local scene, a fire totally destroyed the Red Lion Bar. I almost started to cry on the air. I had stocked the jukebox they had with all these records that I got: Freshmen, Kenton, and Woody Herman stuff. But now my home was gone."

Bobby loved being a disc jockey, playing rock 'n roll records and commercials. But there was a whole lot more to the game than that – contests, promotion and showbiz – the glitz of it. And Don Burdon was a promotion man in his heart. "My one and only radio war was in

Omaha against Don McKinnon," Bobby said. "He was a mother fuckin' jock and a great guy. Now I don't even know what the contest was and I did it. But Burden would stick his head in the booth and say 'give away $5,000 now'. Great. Love to. Ya fuckin' wimp. And then KOWH would up their fuckin' prize." Bobby didn't care much for the contests and hype. But he rolled with it and one Saturday night even had fun with some of it.

Burdon had a promotion going with one of the station's disc jockeys living in and broadcasting from a car. The car was on a platform dangling from a crane 30-feet off the ground about three blocks from Mutual of Omaha. Bobby had been out drinking late, returned home but wasn't tired. "I was feeling like I'd had a couple uppers," he said. "So, I called a cab and go down to see Jim, my disc jockey friend who's on top of his platform. I get out of the fuckin' cab and climb up the fuckin' crane and jump over...ya know, swing over and grab the fuckin'...there was a wire rope around the whole platform so you wouldn't sleep walk and fall off. I get on the fuckin' platform, man, knocked on the window and the poor cat when he heard that, jumped up and hit his fuckin' head on the roof of the car. And he said Bobby what the fuck are you doin' up here, man? And I said I needed a ride home."

"I said I needed a ride home."

Meantime, "Poor Jimmy" started to panic. Bobby had passed out, was asleep on the platform and in danger of rolling off. Jim called the station manager who showed up and talked Bobby down and tried to act natural. "The manager was down on the ground saying, 'act like you're working on something.' But I'm hung over and I knew if I looked down I was going to throw up. I had a fuckin' sport coat on, a shirt, a tie and a topcoat and the manager is sayin' ya got a wrench up there?"

A small crowd had begun to gather and although the station loved publicity, this wasn't it. Slowly, with a hand from Jim on the platform, Bobby made his way down, and into the station manager's car for the ride home. It was Bobby's idea of a good time.

When Monday morning rolled around, Bobby's escapade was topic A, apparently. From the sales room came hysterical laughter. "So I'm on the air," Bobby said, and finally Don Burdon – he was this intense lookin', great lookin' guy, with these Sinatra like eyes, these blue eyes. He sticks his head in the door and says, ya know, Dale, you are the craziest motherfucker I've ever met in my whole fucking life. What are you fucking doing? Then he started to laugh and then I realized that he had told the sales people about what happened."

"Burdon had these meetings," Bobby recalled. "And at one he brought a tape of all the KFWB jocks." KFWB in Los Angeles was a glimpse into Bobby's future. Run by a creative genius named Chuck Blore, KFWB had perfected the art of rock radio. The jocks, production and creative techniques were all top of the line. "We're listening to this tape of KFWB and, of course, it's magnificent," Bobby said. "I mean, everything is right on the fuckin' mark, beautiful jingles. Each dj had a fuckin' theme song. And Burdon says: now that's how I want you fuckers to sound. So I said: Don, maybe if you paid us what they're getting, we'd sound better. Burdon says, I wish you'd confine your thinking to the corner bar. Just go there. Don't ruin these meetings, Dale."

Don Burdon was beginning to get on Bobby's nerves. Burdon loved Bobby on the air but would ride him for forgetting to read promotional copy or sloughing off a minor contest on "secretary's day." Bobby had a solid 44-percent of the audience in the morning and the station was a powerhouse. "You had to stand in line to buy a commercial on that fuckin' station," Bobby said. Bobby thought he should be making more money. "One of the most satisfying things I ever did was in Omaha when I went and asked for a raise and they turned me down," Bobby recalled.

Bobby had already gotten a job offer from Don French the new program director at KDWB in Minneapolis – the Crowell-Collier station, sister to KFWB in Los Angeles and KEWB in San Francisco. Bobby had turned him down. But getting turned down for a raise at KOIL lit Bobby's fuse. "I was so mad I thought, fuck it man," Bobby said. "I walked down to the one stop record distributor they had in Omaha. The guy that ran it was a nice guy and I asked if I could call Minneapolis on his phone. He said, hell yeah, go right ahead. So I called Don French."

It was serendipity. While Bobby was walking to the record distributorship to make his call, Don French had been calling the radio station for Bobby to make another job offer. French thought Bobby was returning his call, made an offer of $12,000 dollars; Bobby accepted and the deal was done. Back at KOIL, Bobby walked into the General Manager's office and gave his two weeks notice. "I mean, it was the sweetest fuckin'...it would have been sweeter had I known Don had called me," Bobby said. "Don told me later that he would have gone up to $15,000 to get me."

It was good news and bad for Todd Storz. Bobby Dale would be out of their hair in Omaha but WDGY, the Storz powerhouse in Minneapolis, was about to get blown out of the water.

12 The Turning Point

"...KDWB was on its way to becoming number one."

Back in Minneapolis, setting the stage for Bobby's biggest break was a clutch of creative people transforming a failed radio station into the talk of the town.

Sam Sherwood, a WISK disc jockey, who would stay on with the new Crowell-Collier operation to be called KDWB, recalled the day in September of '59 when "KDWB Color Radio" began taking shape. "A week before airtime, one of those fancy airport rental cars came, sending up a cloud of Radio Road gravel," he said. "Out leaped a slick programming top gun by the name of Chuck Blore. It was like shaking hands with an electric socket."

Bob Purcell, Crowell-Collier president was right behind him, and then along came this chap from Texas by the name of Don French – KDWB's new program director. Sherwood said, "French was as warm as a slice of granny apple and fully equipped with a quart container, three quarters empty of Vladimir's finest vodka. No matter where the mark was on the bottle, you could never tell whether Don was drinking it or the bottle leaked."

And all of a sudden WISK took a jolt of creativity the likes of which Sherwood said he'd never witnessed. "With Chuck and Don, the studios and hallways just got filled to the brim with ideas, promotions and excitement,"

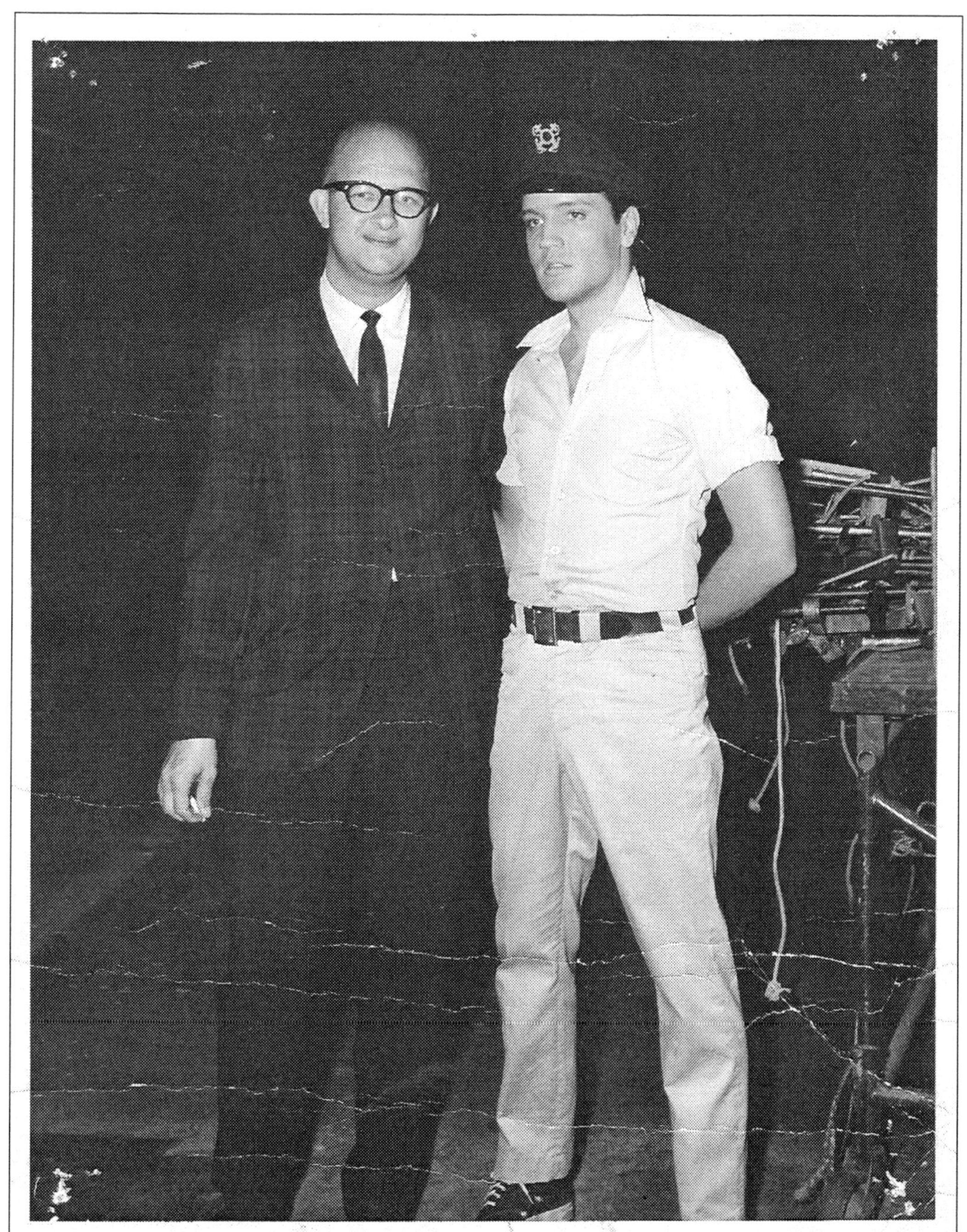

Bobby always loved his photo with "The King".

Sherwood said. "Big time jocks were heading in from all points on the map. Hal Murray, the morning comedian jumped on a bus from Houston, Texas. Bob Chasteen blew in from Chicago, Phil Page a late arrival from Texas, and Charlie "Hollywood" Arlington was there to set up a news department."

Don French was still working on getting Bobby Dale to join the team.

Todd Storz and Gordon McClendon got the rock 'n roll radio revolution underway, but it was the creative programming genius of Blore that would take it the next step. Blore was a disc jockey and program director under Gordon McClendon at KTSA in San Antonio and KELP in Dallas. He was hired by Bob Purcell, the GM at KFWB to produce those famous jingles that made such an impression on Bobby and bring "Color Radio" as he called it, to Los Angeles, San Francisco and Minneapolis.

Blore recognized that teenagers who went crazy for rock 'n roll radio in the mid-50's, were growing up and that the popular radio format needed to grow with them to appeal to a wider audience. In his internet memoir *Okay, Okay, I Wrote the Book,* Blore is asked by Bob Sande and Larry Greene – the guys commissioned to produce the KFWB jingles – what his idea was. What is "Color Radio," they asked. Blore's reply: "It's an incredibly entertaining team of deejays, each with a distinctive and appealing personality and it's a stream of content unlike anything you've ever heard before. It's programming that could change the sound of radio forever."

KFWB's "Color Radio" experiment got underway January 2nd, 1958 and "color channel 98," as it was called, quickly became Southern California's number one radio station, and was just as quickly copied by radio stations around the country.

The failing WISK morphed into KDWB that September by first playing the French version of the Coasters hit *Charlie Brown* and only that record, over and over for the first 24-hours. The newspapers got wind of it. That drew the intended attention and KDWB was off and running with Chuck Blore at quarterback.

Blore had purchased saturation radio advertising for a product called "Formula 63," guaranteed to relieve the blues. The spots were created by the man who made Hadacol famous. Hadacol was an elixir marketed as a vitamin supplement that contained 12 percent alcohol and was quite popular in the dry counties of the south. Drug stores throughout the Minneapolis-St. Paul area were stocked with a "limited free supply" of "Formula 63." It didn't matter which radio station you were listening

> ***"It's programming that could change the sound of radio forever."***

to, there was the famous voice telling you, "I'm the fellow who brought you Hadacol and I've got something good for you." The drug stores were flooded with folks getting their free sample while supplies last. Inside was the cure for "ennui" – that feeling of utter weariness and discontent resulting from satiety or lack of interest, boredom – as the dictionary describes it. They were told to tune into 63 on the radio dial and their problems would be solved. Meanwhile KDWB played its promotion stinger, recorded by Charles Arlington: "63, that's easy to remember" – in nearly every break between records. It took a while for competing radio stations to catch on. A WLOL disc jockey stopped in a Snyders Drug Store for a pack of smokes, spotted the "Formula 63," read the KDWB propaganda and blew the whistle. Some were shaking their heads, others were pissed off, but by then the damage was done and KDWB was on its way to becoming number one.

13 The Way Back Home

Bobby didn't care much for airplane rides, but after getting the KDWB offer he flew to Minneapolis to meet his new boss, Don French. Throughout his career, Bobby would reflect on his friendship with Don French with affection. "He was such a groovy dude," Bobby said. "Just the sweetest man I ever met in my fuckin' life. That weekend was the first time I ever met him. And, of course, I fell in love with him." There was an obvious and immediate special bond between the two men. They laughed a lot and enjoyed each others company. As a boss, Don made it easy on Bobby. "The only thing he ever said to me about bein' a jock – he said Bobby, the only thing I worry about is sometimes you go over people's heads. And I said, my God, really? Not bad for a practically high school dropout."

That first weekend Don picked Bobby up at the airport and headed to a hotel where they hooked up with Dick LaPalm, a Chicago record promotion man who'd worked for Nat King Cole at one time. "I liked Dick," Bobby said. "I liked a lot of those promo people. They were hard workers." And most of those promo people liked Bobby. There was a lot of mutual back scratching going on between record promoters and disc jockeys. It was Bob Serempa – the Minneapolis record distributor

"Bobby was going home."

who'd bailed Bobby out that drunken Saturday night – who put the bug in Don French's ear about Bobby's talent. Serempa covered a five state area in the Midwest and was well aware of the lay of his land. Dick LaPalm, too, knew all the jocks and their program directors. It was important to be a member in good standing of that club. And I'm certain LaPalm picked up the tab that night at the hotel. And what a tab it must have been. "We got loaded," Bobby said. "We got bombed out of our minds on booze, and I flew back to Omaha."

From the drawing boards at the Brown Institute of the Air, through Glendive, Montana, Fargo and Omaha in four years, Bobby was going home. His family, friends and former girlfriend would all be there. Bobby would say later, "It was strange workin' in a market where you'd lived."

Bobby's boyhood friend, Jim Watkins said Bobby had a great desire to be somebody. "We'd walk together late at night on our way home and Bobby'd say, I'm gonna make it sometime, Jimmy. I'm gonna be famous."

Bobby's few public appearances were sheer torture for him.

(Left to right): Randy Cook, Dick Halvorson, Bobby Dale, Sam Sherwood, Bob Friend, Lou Riegert-Waters and Hal Murray

14

A Swingin' Gentleman

"...one of the KDWB 'Seven Swingin' Gentlemen'."

Bobby hated the first day of his Minneapolis homecoming in January, 1960. "The day I left Omaha there was this huge fuckin' blizzard," Bobby said. "I didn't have a car, of course, so I took a train…got a sleeper…fuckin' great…on my way to the new job…and crazy Don. We arrive at the train depot in Minneapolis. Don is there to meet me."

Don French's initial promotion gimmick for Bobby was simple, but it drove Bobby nuts. From the train depot, Don took Bobby to the airport and handed him a round trip ticket to Rochester, Minnesota. Bobby quickly changed planes in Rochester, flew back to Minneapolis. And at the airport, there was Don waiting with a huge group of folks. "They were listeners who were greeting me at the fuckin' airport," Bobby said. "And I thought, oh god, I hate this kinda shit."

It was the kinda shit Bobby would have to get used to. He had officially become one of the KDWB "Seven Swingin' Gentlemen." That's what Chuck Blore called his deejays.

And if there was one thing Crowell Collier Broadcasting and its leader, Chuck Blore, loved to do was promote the deejays in all sorts of ways that Bobby hated. He would have to get used to it. As much as he loved playing records on the radio, the radio promotion gimmicks that irritated him so much in Omaha would soon seem like child's play.

Author: Lou Riegert was my name in 1960. I became Lou Waters after moving to San Francisco in the mid 60's. What follows is a personal note.

Writing this story now reminds me of my own radio journey and how it intersected with "The Wide, Weird World of Bobby Dale." I grew up with WDGY while attending suburban Minneapolis High Schools. In the afternoons I'd listen to Tom Wynn on "WeeGee" as the station was unfortunately nicknamed. Wynn's enthusiasm was infectious and I'd get caught up in the idea of how much fun it must be to work on the radio. In college, at the University of Minnesota while studying Architectural Engineering, I discovered the campus radio station, WMMR. Several local deejays helped run the place. It was closed circuit radio for the dormitories. It was ABC affiliated. We carried Paul Harvey News at noon, followed by the 15-minute variety shtick of Brad Johnson and Morrie Carlson, on a program they called "The Five Minute Program That Runs Ten Minutes Overtime." It was 15 minutes of anything goes and it was pure fun. I became hopelessly addicted to radio. My architectural studies suffered a major blow as I devoted nearly full time to WMMR. I became the news director, sent out a tape to WMIN, a local radio station. I got a part-time job, announcing time, temperature, reading commercials, news casts. Five bucks-an-hour, but I was "in radio." I put my slide rule in a drawer and never looked back. Two months later, AFTRA – our union, went on strike. All of a sudden I was "out of radio." I was on the street carrying an "unfair" protest sign on a stick wondering why I'd let my architectural studies slide.

In the picket line was an announcer named Dick Driscoll. He told me about WISK and that it was changing call letters and becoming a rock station. He said I should check it out. I did. I later learned it's mostly about timing in this business. They needed a weekend disc jockey and part time newsman. I got the job and my big chance. I was in on the ground floor with a unique opportunity to watch and be a part of a rock and roll powerhouse operation come to life.

And now with the addition of Bobby Dale as afternoon drive time jock, 3 to 6pm, there were Seven Swingin' Gentlemen. A special song was written and performed in Los Angeles including the names of all the jocks – Hal Murray in morning drive, Phil Page nine until noon, Sam Sherwood noon to 3pm, Bobby Dale afternoon drive, Bob Friend 6 to nine pm, Randy Cook nine to midnight and Dick Halvorson on the all night shift, and me on the weekends. We were good to go against Todd Storz's WDGY operation – my teenage home for rock 'n roll. And then something shocking happened. Phil Page, the morning guy,

"...Bobby Dale was unique."

We were everywhere-on the radio, bus benches and billboards.

I was Lou Riegert before I was Lou Waters.

got fired. I never knew why. But Don French quickly shuffled the deejays, moving Bob Friend into Pages spot and me into Bob Friend's 6 to 9pm slot. I officially became a "Swingin' Gentleman." I was also a 21-year-old greenhorn amid veteran disc jockeys. They were all great dj's but Bobby Dale was unique. It all came naturally to him. He loved the music. He was funny both on and off the air. He fascinated me.

I was raised in an upper middle income Catholic family, toed the line, an honor student in high school and attended the University of Minnesota as an architectural engineering student. Bobby was raised during the depression and spent most of his teenage years on the street or in jail. We couldn't have been more different. But I didn't know all that at the time.

It wasn't long before I got to know the man. And it changed my life in significant ways.

15

Scotch and Don Juan in Hell

"Bobby was at the bar twirling a smoldering Kool...."

Just before 9pm on a Friday night as I, Lou Riegert the disc jockey, was wrapping up my furious 3-hours of "colorful" radio chatter and rock 'n roll, the hotline lit up. It was Bobby. Did I want to stop by Conroy's – just down the road from the station – and have a drink with him? With the exception of Don French, Bobby didn't socialize with the station's disc jockeys. I was surprised at the call and was about to get an education in the fine art of getting drunk.

Bobby was at the bar twirling a smoldering Kool unfiltered cigarette between his thumb and index finger, a habit of his. In front of him was a tall glass of what I later learned was Cutty Sark and water. It was his favorite beverage. He hadn't touched it. After a few minutes, he slammed it back in one motion, ordered another and was off and running. I was not a drinker but I tried one of those Cutty Sark's and after getting past the awful taste of the first one, began feeling goofy. Bobby seemed to be getting a kick out of watching me lose a vestige of my virginity which I continued losing right up until closing time. Bobby wanted me to come back to his apartment. We went and my Bobby Dale music appreciation experience got underway.

I had always loved music. My Dad was a professional musician in the forties, playing

baritone and alto sax on the weekends at the area ballrooms with the "Red Pepper Orchestra." I took piano lessons for eight years and played clarinet in the high school and city bands. I had a great appreciation for the big bands but was not a student of musical history, until the nights at Bobby's place after the bars closed.

At work, we played what modern popular music had become – 40 or 50 songs on the charts repeated endlessly 24 hours a day. At Bobby's we listened to Billie Holiday, Illinois Jaquet, Fats Waller, Sarah Vaughn, Sinatra, Lester Young, Ella Fitzgerald and Duke Ellington.

Some nights we'd listen to George Bernard Shaw's *Don Juan in Hell* – a Columbia masterwork recording featuring Charles Boyer, Charles Laughton, Cedric Hardwicke and Agnes Moorehead. I began getting a sense there was a whole lot more to Bobby Dale than meets the eye. He knew his music, loved listening to it, telling me about its origins, and paying particular attention to whether I was getting it – appreciating the beauty pouring out of his vast and varied array of stolen albums. He was deejay by day and deejay by night. I liked them both.

KDWB's transmitter site, from which we broadcast, was a one story, slump block building located down dusty Radio Road. It was in the middle of nowhere – east of St. Paul about 12 miles from the Wisconsin border, in the middle of hundreds of empty acres of farmland all around. In fact the station had been previously owned by three brothers who chose the call letters WCOW. When record promoters would bring recording artists out for lunch, there was considerable talk of our remote location. "So this is the home of color radio," they'd say. "Sweet." But you go where the action is and that was us, and the record guys would flock to us in a steady stream.

Bobby, of course, was the music director. He'd screen all the new records coming in and nearly every day I'd see him in the tiny closet-like music room with a stack of 45 rpm's on his arm, listening to one after the other, never listening for long. He'd make his picks, then once a week all the deejays would meet to get marching orders, critiques and a chance to hear the new music. Bobby would play the records, the jocks would offer their two cents worth and we'd vote. Some records voted down would reappear week after week if pressure from the record companies was great enough. But Bobby usually was the final say on what a hit was and what was not. We all trusted his "ear" including Don French.

"Don trusted me with the music almost totally," Bobby said. "The only reason I had used that record *Apache* was 'cuz I read about it in Bill Gavin's sheet in 1960." Bill Gavin's San Francisco based "sheet" would arrive once a week and provide music tips and research and often far outweighed the information found in music trade journals. Bobby kept close tabs on what Gavin had to say.

"I loved the record *Apache* and we started playing it," Bobby recalled. "French called and said Bobby, maybe I'll regret this but I have to ask you to take that record off the air. And I said, Don please tell me you're kidding. He said, Bobby I'm not kidding. I said, I'll tell you what – I will, of course, do it but I want you to acknowledge now that when you come up to me and apologize...if I don't talk to you, you'll know why. And he said...do you really think...and I said Don, it isn't a matter of what I think...it's a smash, ya know? And he said, Jesus Christ...really?" Don never argued with Bobby about a record again.

Bobby's special talent was hearing a lyric, remembering it and recognizing its emotional impact on a music audience. Bobby, for all his bluster and humor, was a pool of emotions reflected in his tastes in music and film. "The one that used to tear me up was *Meet Me in St. Louis*, Bobby recalled, when Judy Garland would sing to Margaret O'Brien when they were lifting their roots, getting ready to leave St. Louis and move to New York...and Garland's got this little music box, she starts turning it...ya know, the little tinkle, and then sings *Have Yourself a Merry Little Christmas.* What an incredible song."

How did this love affair with music begin? "Well, I can remember the first record, babe, when I was in grade school. I had a

"He was deejay by day and deejay by night."

recording of *Darling Jevousem Boucoup* by Hildegard. I couldn't wait to rush home from grade school with that fuckin' thing, man. I always loved music. Stan Kenton and Woody Herman were the first two big ones in my life. This is long before radio. When I got into radio, I could hear black music especially because that's what I fuckin' listened to so much. Not consciously. I said this is jazz music, and jazz music is what I like. You mention to somebody you like this kinda music and they'd say you gotta hear Charlie Parker. He's the man. He was the man, period. He recorded at that time on Dial records which, in those days, cost a dollar-and-five-cents for a 78 rpm. I had a record player and a lot of jazz records – Gillespie, Parker and Miles and when we went on a streetcar or sumpthin' and had our albums, they'd always be picture out, man, so everybody'd know how cool we were at 15 and 16."

Later on, "Bobby's gang" would listen to Tchaikovsky, Rimsky-Korsakov, Stravinsky, and Strauss. Miles Davis was still in the mix. Jazz was the thing. But the play list expanded to include Illinois Jaquet and Flip Phillips who were the two big tenor players in Bobby's life just then. So when he finally got out of Glen Lake, on probation, and entered 12th grade, Bobby joined the South High School Band and started learning to play tenor sax. Bobby asked his folks for money to buy the sax. Bobby said, "They would have bought me anything to keep me from getting in trouble again." His parents sacrificed again for their Babe.

Bobby was thrilled when he got the tenor sax. "But then," he said, "I realized I had to practice, and it was such a fuckin' drag. It was interfering with my listening." The band teacher told him, "if you want to play like Jaquet, Phillips and Lester Young, you've got to remember they just didn't pick up an instrument and blow it. They paid their dues. They practiced."

Bobby's attention to lyric was no less acute while listening to the records vying to become part of Billboard Magazine's top 100 or any Rock stations Top 40. When measured against the number of records being produced at the time, the chance of a record's success was slim to none. With certain songs, Bobby's passion and sensibilities were blood raw.

"Whenever I see one of these Rock 'n Roll shows, they had one claiming nobody wanted to play black music. I said, Christ that's all they played. If you were playing the Top 40 – based on a national list – then that's what you played, especially in '56 and '57. It was a way of life."

Bobby had a special bone to pick with Mitch Miller, who in 1959 was the head of A&R – artists and repertoire – at Columbia records for some of their biggest hits, Frankie Lane hits for instance. Johnnie Ray's *Walkin' in the Rain.* Miller was not a fan of Rock 'n Roll radio. He said the music played on the radio was was the worst – for 9, 10 and eleven year olds. "He did not like black music," Bobby said. "He didn't like the R&B. When he heard records like *Get a Job* by the Silhouettes, he didn't fuckin' understand, man. He never really listened to the lyric: "Get a job that I never could find." I thought that that was one of the most incredible protest songs that nobody ever knew. Steve Allen recited it, making fun of it on his TV show. And I'm thinkin', Jesus Christ, man. He's a very intelligent man, very aware, very humane, and he hasn't got a fuckin' clue. How could you not understand? 'The woman throws the want ads right my way, and never fails to say…was there any work for you today? Yip yip yip yip yip…get a job.' No fuckin' doubt about it, man. Super heavy."

Bobby was part of the protest in 1953 down at the Jiffy Car Wash. "I walked in wearing a nice navy blue overcoat, double breasted, a really neat coat," Bobby recalled. "I didn't look like a guy that'd be goin' to work in a car wash. The owner and foreman were white. All the laborers were black – two kinds of blacks - transients who were in and out in a few days, and family men who couldn't find other jobs. I saw a couple musicians that I knew. I mean, I knew their work. I worked there until we went on strike."

Jiffy Car Wash decided to cut the hourly wage from a-dollar-and-a-quarter to one-dollar-an-hour. "These men had to do fuckin' something, man," Bobby said. "The main black guy, the unofficial leader, Russ Everett, said let's wait until a beautiful day in May. So we did, and it was on a Saturday with cars lined up for blocks. Russell said strip off your uniforms, told the owner we quit. We walked off, got some booze, went out by Lake Calhoun, sat in the sun and got drunk." Bobby was back in his element. And very soon he'd have to get another job.

16 Stories He'd Tell

"It's Saturday morning in the Twin Cities, ya know?"

Radio was a comfortable place for Bobby Dale. The cast of colorful characters was an endless source of conflict and amusement. The players came from all backgrounds, had a unique talent for entertaining and each were flawed in amusing and sometimes disturbing ways. It was an all male fraternity of jocks competing for attention in the high speed, energy driven arena of what had become known as the "Rock 'n Roll Revolution." Rock 'n Roll was here to stay as the story went. But the "Revolution" was, in fact, an evolution in modern popular music made all the more powerful and pronounced by the millions of Baby Boomer teens who were driving the market as they always had and would for generations to come.

The disc jockeys were the glue holding the various Top 40 formats together and the best disc jockeys were the ones who attracted the largest audiences. Chuck Blore's formula – "incredibly entertaining team of deejays, each with a distinctive and appealing personality and a stream of content unlike anything you've ever heard before" – had become the envy of the modern radio industry.

In Minneapolis, one of our incredibly entertaining personalities was an irascible Jewish fellow from Texas known as Hal Murray. Armed with shoe boxes full of Robert Orben joke books and a gift of gab that couldn't help but grab attention, Hal Murray and his "Murray-go-Round" became the number one morning show in the Twin Cities. Hal's play on words and corny jokes took the town by storm. He made his Jewishness part of the act.

Bobby recalled a story told to him by Art Nelson, a great disc jockey who worked with Hal at a McClendon station in Texas. As Bobby retold the story, "Art Nelson is playing poker with some of the other jocks and they're listening to Hal Murray who's doing the all night show. There was supposed to be a taped news intro. It didn't work. Hal says the heck with it and started to give the news. Well, at the time, the Air Force was trying to recover a nose cone from some space shot, and in the middle of this newscast about this nosecone, Hal says – I used to know a friend of mine – so and so – some Jewish name he gave, and he had a nose like a cone. Then he started the weather, and then that taped news intro came plowing over everything. Art said there were maybe six people at this table and they had to quit for almost a half hour. I knew a guy named Cohn and he had a funny nose. Jesus. One of my favorite all time radio stories."

"I notice you never laugh at my jokes."

That was Hal. He was our morning man and because he was, he rose very early to shine at 6am until 9am. At 10am once a week we'd hold our music meetings to decide the fate of records Bobby had chosen for consideration. Invariably Hal would fall asleep sitting up. Morning shows took a lot out of him, apparently. The most memorable meeting was the one during which the entire on-air staff tiptoed from the room, records and all and held our get together down the hall. Hal was furious. That was Hal. He often got furious, mostly in jealous competition with Bobby Dale. And the stories were legend.

We worked with engineers in the beginning. They were the guys with F.C.C. licenses to monitor the transmitter site where we worked. They ran the commercial breaks. That left the jock separated from the engineer by plate glass in a booth with two turntables, a microphone, and an intercom switch to communicate with his engineer in the control room. Picture that while Bobby tells another Hal story. "The engineer was a guy named Gary something – a stocky guy. I liked Gary a lot and he loved me on the air. He was working with Hal that day and Carol and I were listening as we drove out of town on a short vacation. Suddenly there was total silence, man. I mean nothing. Not a sound. And this went on for about five minutes. Later I found out that Hal had said to Gary, I notice that you never laugh at my jokes, and Gary said you're not funny – you oughta be funny like Bobby Dale and Hal got in a physical fight with the guy. And after the silence, Hal finally came back on breathing heavily and its like, "It's Saturday morning in the Twin Cities, ya know?"

Hal and Bobby would fight more battles together at KFWB, farther down the road less traveled. But before heading west, Bobby Dale had a wedding to attend, his own. Charlie Boone, who would be his best man, said Bobby was a sensitive and lonely guy. And Bobby said, "Yeah I'm sure that's why I got married." Bobby had pined for Carol and he finally won her over. "This is the classic example of be careful what you wish for, because you might get it, man. That doesn't sound fair, but she was the first love of my life and the only one that I knew that shared any interest in me, other than putting in an order for a stolen sweater or something."

But the wedding was on and it was over almost before it started.

17 Wedding Bell Blues

"Robert Dale Bastiensen was headed for 'the big time'."

Bobby and Carol Johnson were married September 17, 1960, nearly nine years after they met. When I asked Bobby if Charlie Boone was his best man, he replied, "absolutely…I guess," followed by peals of laughter.

"I can tell you in all honesty…that Saturday morning…that day that I got married…I remember I was lying on the bed in my bedroom and I kept thinkin' what the fuck am I doin'? I finally get somewhere in life where I wasn't sleeping in a friends car or turning up on their couch. Suddenly I knew, even before I said I do, that I shouldn't. But it's a little late, ya know?"

After the ceremony it was off to the bar with Charlie to get a drink. Carol had to go looking for Bobby and it wouldn't be the last time she'd wonder where her husband was and what he was doing. Carol recalled that day, "We were to have lunch after the wedding with 13 or 14 people and then go on a honeymoon. Bobby disappeared. We got into the hotel. He was gone. My mother was mad saying, no bride should be alone on her wedding day. I don't know where he went. He came back later and we had dinner at the hotel. It took awhile before he softened up."

Bobby did soften up and before the end of the year, Carol was pregnant. Three years

Bobby sunbathing with his first love, Carol.

later Bobby would tell Carol he didn't want to be married anymore and that he knew it wasn't what he wanted from the time he went out for a drink with Charlie, his best man, immediately following the wedding ceremony. Before he would lose "the love of his life" forever, Bobby's radio life would change radically, and his Midwestern days would end. Robert Dale Bastiensen was headed for "the big time."

18

Hooray for Hollywood

"California dreamin' became a nightmare."

July, 1961: KFWB Radio newsmen go on strike and drag the number one rated disc jockeys along with them in sympathy. Bobby Dale and Hal Murray got the word they were being transferred to Los Angeles to help fill the gaping holes created by the striking dj's. B. Mitchell Reed, one of the top KFWB jocks would head to Minneapolis to take Bobby's 3-6pm drive-time shift. The die was being cast for the most regrettable experience in Bobby Dale's professional life. He would get the nine-to-midnight shift at the number one station in the nation's second largest market. He would be making more money than he ever had and record promotion people would be hanging out in bars with him and picking up the tab. "My life's ambition," Bobby said.

The rest of it was a hornet's nest of resentment, ridicule and retaliation. The on-air staff was on the street banking on a quick and easy solution to grievances, planning on returning to work and continued dominance in the L.A. radio market. It didn't turn out that way. In 1961, KFWB did have a phenomenal reputation, not only in Los Angeles, but around the country. Disc jockeys of all shapes and sizes would crawl through crushed glass to work there, and that was part of the problem. Replacing the striking newsmen and their sym-

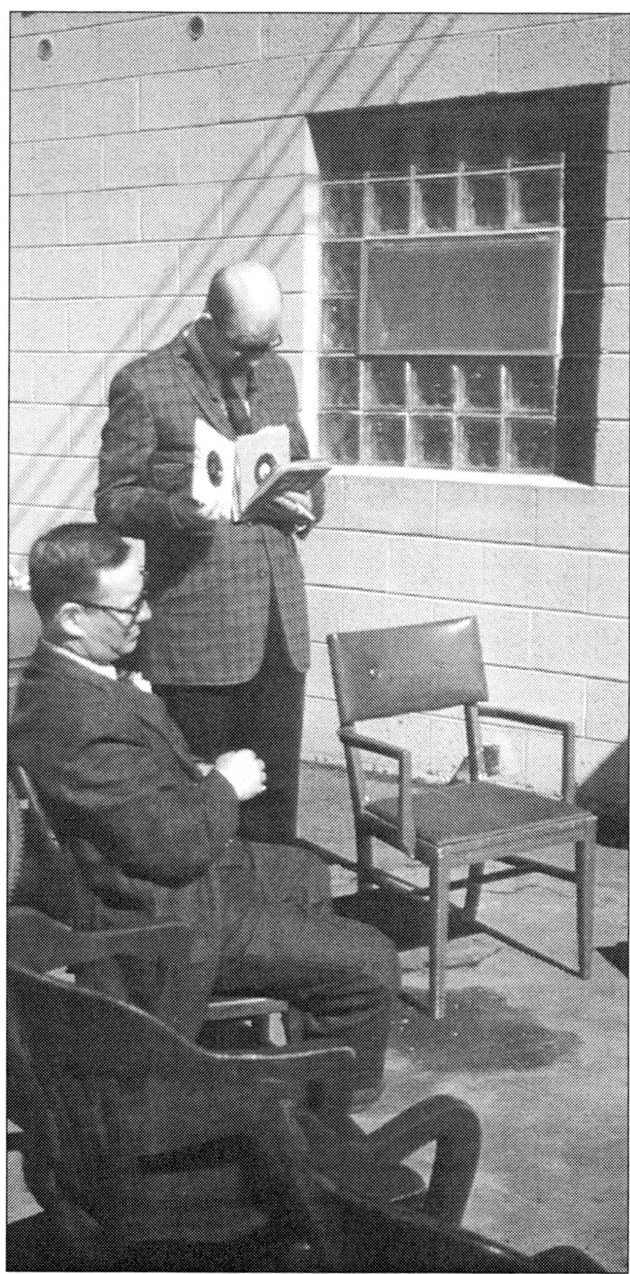

Hal Murray about to doze as Bobby sorts records for the weekly meeting.

pathetic dj's colleagues was not a huge problem. It prolonged the strike, and created hard feelings which, according to Bobby, was the beginning of the end of KFWB and its Crowell Collier affiliates KDWB in Minneapolis and KEWB in San Francisco. It was into this mess Bobby advanced his career in the turbulent rock 'n roll wars of California. Bobby was about to become a scab and things were about to get very nasty.

Bobby interviews June Christy in Minneapolis.

19 Channel 98

"I didn't have a big desire to live and work in L.A."

The hassles began almost immediately.
"I went to L.A. in July, 1961," Bobby recalled. "I finished my show at 6 o'clock in Minneapolis and the newsroom guy drove Hal Murray, his wife, Carol and me to the airport. We got on the flight. We were first class – champagne and steak – and landed in L.A. at 9:30 and headed for the Knickerbocker Hotel. The guy at the desk says which one is Bobby Dale and hands me the key – to a suite." Hal was given a smaller room and Bobby didn't hear the end of it for days.

"I was already wishing I hadn't made the decision to live in L.A.," Bobby said. I didn't have a big desire to live and work there, although, of course, it was the place to be." It was the place where Bobby's natural gifts for music and comic observation had gotten him just 5 years after he decided to get a job in radio. The media politics was another matter. Bobby wanted no part of that. But he was about to get a crash course in how the game of rock 'n roll radio was played and how little fun it could be.

The first order of business: head for Hollywood Boulevard and a meeting with Chuck Blore, the boss. KFWB was located on Hollywood Boulevard near Vine where it's been said everyone in the world passed by at least once. Bobby led the way up the Avenue of Stars with Hal Murray at his heel. The AFTRA picket line loomed large and Bobby considered heading for home. But the thrill of anticipation took over and, averting their eyes, Bobby and Hal skipped past the strikers, up a flight of stairs and into KFWB's studio, a downsized bit of rock 'n roll territory, but in L.A., the center of the universe. "Number-One" screamed the Sandy and Greene jingle through the monitors as Bobby and Hal bounded up the stairs, not quite sure if they'd be hit by thrown garbage or worse. Crossing a picket line wasn't in the radio handbook back at the Brown Institute in Minneapolis. This was uncharted territory.

"Patti Page was in Blore's office when Hal and I showed up," Bobby recalled. "She wanted to get the hell out of there without the hassle of crossing the picket line, and I can't blame her for that."

Bobby and Hal got their marching orders: Hal would do mornings, replacing Gary Owens, one of the best morning men in the business. Bobby worked 9 to midnight, exchanging places with B. Mitchell Reed who rode the red eye to Minneapolis to take over Bobby's afternoon drive shift at KDWB.

Mitch Reed – BMR he called himself – talked himself out of a political science career "for the boogie and glamour of broadcasting."

Mitch Reed had a jazz soul, having worked the all nights at WOR in New York on

"Patti Page was in Blore's office when Hal and I showed up."

his "Birdland Jazz Show" and his hip style worked well in the Top 40 format when he became one of the original "Seven Swingin' Gentlemen" of "Color Radio KFWB." He enjoyed and had great fun with it. He wouldn't be in Minneapolis long but he literally threw himself into the station and the city and was received with great affection.

In Los Angeles, the strike was simple arithmetic. The KFWB newsmen walked out. They just wanted a better deal. Somehow they talked the disc jockeys into honoring their picket line. So the jocks went on sympathy strike. The engineers, the guys who kept the station on the air did not honor the picket line. Bobby said, "If you coulda pulled those engineers out of there, you might have had a chance to win that fuckin' battle. But you're not gonna have any trouble getting dj's, are you kiddin'? And newsmen…you know."

As Bobby and others saw it grind on, it was a losing situation. And when the men on the picket line realized it, the meltdown began.

Ted Quillan, a young, brilliant KFWB jock, was on top of his world and he was about to slide off.

Bobby had a thing about Ted Quillan. He said, "I just loved the cat." He was a character. Bobby was a fan. He'd listen to Quillan's all night show. "When he did the show, Bobby recalled, "after two in the morning, you didn't hear a single pop record. You heard Count Basie, Francis Faye, Mel Torme and he would have a fifth of gin with him and a hooker and a gun, man. In fact, when I got put on the all night show on KFWB, one night there's a buzz at the back and it was Ted Quillan. He comes in and he's got this really great London Fog lookin' trench coat and he pulls out a fifth of gin and these ribs…and a .38. He slaps it all down in the booth. And I said, Ted that's very nice of you but I don't drink while I'm workin', especially not on the all night show. He said, really? I never would have made it through one."

Quillan, when asked about his breach of Top 40 playlist etiquette made no apologies. He said, "I called it blues for breakfast." And he was never called on it.

Bobby said Chuck Blore's philosophy was: if I don't listen I don't know about it. And so Blore let it go and by 5 in the morning Quillan would be back on the Top 40 playlist, feeling no pain.

Bobby was always baffled how the KFWB disc jockeys got snookered into supporting the striking newsmen by walking out. Ted Quillan recalled it vividly: "I was some redneck kid outta Texas and they said if you don't go out on strike we're gonna black ball ya, and you'll never get a job. I said ok. That scared me. So I went out and that's when Bobby came in."

When the strike was settled a month later, it was not a matter of all is forgiven, c'mon back; we'll be one big happy family again. Quillan said it didn't happen that way. He said there was sniping all around. He was upset about being treated like a kid and told Bob Purcell, the General Manager, to either handle the snarl in which he found himself or pay off his contract. Quillan said, "They paid off my contract and I left."

And he left in a big way, first aboard a slow German Freighter, programming a pirate radio station off Denmark and in his trusty Rambler, toured much of Europe. Upon his return to L.A. in late 1962, he was immediately offered a job at KRLA – KFWB's deadliest Top 40 rival. He would be one of the powerful instruments employed in knocking off KFWB.

While Quillan was on sabbatical in his Rambler, Bobby stayed on at KFWB when the strike ended, keeping his head down, not sure how or if the returning disc jockeys would accept him. Quillan said he bore no ill will against any jock who crossed the line. "It was just business goin' down as far as I knew," he said.

Bill Balance, one of the returning jocks was not so circumspect. He lost his 9-midnight shift to Bobby, who was offered any spot he wanted on any of the three Crowell Collier stations. Bobby picked L.A., got Balance's shift and began weathering the slings and arrows of bruised egos and hard feelings.

The Los Angeles Rock 'n Roll Radio war was especially intense with big money giveaways to lure an audience, to just plain fraud. One particularly public scandal lit a fuse that exploded in all directions: it was a KRLA contest worth $50,000 dollars if you could walk up to the new KRLA disc jockey and say, "are you Perry Allen?"

Meanwhile, over at KFWB, the "news guy" – as Bobby called him – Charles Arlington, a friend of Perry Allen, heard of the contest and knew his friend was still on the radio in Buffalo and hadn't yet left for L.A. Arlington and others boarded a plane for Buffalo, drove to the radio station where Perry Allen worked. One of the KFWB staffers walked up to the man and asked, "Are you Perry Allen? He said, "Why yes I am." The staffer said, "That's great. I want my $50,000 dollars." And KRLA had to pay up.

Bobby remembered the incident well. "There was a fuckin' picture in the L.A. paper of Crowell-Collier, KFWB'S parent, getting the check for $50,000 dollars and donating it to charity. But that, of course, infuriated the guys who owned KRLA and they started taping Bill Balance."

By today's standards, it might seem tame, but in the early 60's Bill Balance, an enormously talented disc jockey had a "blue problem." Bobby said, "He would be a multi-millionaire today if he was on the air and allowed to do what he was best able to do – which was talk dirty. You know: my girlfriend is like an old screen door she's been banged so many times."

Balance was popular, but the problem was KRLA was taping it all and sending separate copies to the seven members of the Federal Communications Commission. KFWB was forced to limit Balance's gig to Saturday nights only, six to midnight and all on tape. As Bobby put it, "it was all because of his mouth."

Bobby ended up with Balance's prime 9 to midnight weekday shift, "Bill Balance was my nemesis in L.A.," Bobby said. "He'd get drunk, call me up and threaten me. He'd say you fuckin' son-of-a-bitch, I'm comin' down there, and this guy was a judo instructor in the fuckin' Marine Corps. He was no one to fuck with. He was a jerk." Bobby never liked confrontation.

Years later at KRLA Bobby was the 6 to midnight jock, Bill Balance did the overnights. Bobby said, "I was never any good at holding a grudge against people, man, ya know, so we'd be playing stuff like *I Heard it Through the Grapevine* by Creedence and I told Balance, I said look, I've got this Creedence album and the *Grapevine* cut is 11 minutes long. He said you're kidding. I said no, it's the all night show, why not play some of these long records. So that's what he did. I gave him quite a few albums. They would cut down those songs, of course, for Top 40 radio. I didn't win him over, but we got along o.k."

Bobby just wanted to get along. His teenage experiences taught him what confrontation could lead to. Balance's threats of violence were not what he signed on for. But Bobby could see the humor in this contest of ill will.

"There was one funny thing that happened when my brother Pete was art director for Cambell Methune and Hamm's Beer," Bobby said. "Pete's the guy who wandered into a Hamm's Beer TV commercial, taking a napkin, and drawing a bear on it. Then he turns around and the Bear comes to life. That was his concept. Pete would come to L.A. to help out with the advertising. They were auditioning people for voice overs and Balance was there. When my brother, Pete, saw Bill Balance from KFWB, he walked up to him and said you're Bill Balance? Well, he said I'm Bobby Dale's brother. My name's Pete Bastiensen. Balance said, well that's your problem." Balance didn't get the Hamm's beer voice over job, incidentally. Bobby would just have to live with Balance's anger.

Bobby's next hurdle was adjusting to his new life in L.A. KFWB was more that just a rock 'n roll radio station. It was not only the number one rock 'n roll radio station in the second largest market in the country, it had the power to control airplay and sales of millions of hit records and often a record became a hit only if KFWB decided to get on board.

Chuck Blore appointed Bobby, Ted Randall and record librarian Gloria Clark as part of a KFWB music committee that listened to the new record releases. The committee would then determine which records would be presented at the weekly meeting attended by all. Bobby picked the records he knew would be hits. Randall took care of the rest. Of Ted Randall, Bobby said, "He could hear shit I couldn't stand – like *Johnny Angel* by Shelley Fabares."

"He'd get drunk, call me up and threaten me."

The first meeting after the strike ended was attended by all the jocks who'd been on strike and those who crossed the picket line. "They were all sitting in the same room, Bobby said, and I had to play the records. If you even got to play 10-seconds of a fuckin' record, it was amazing. They would all, naw, fuck it." It was a bumpy transition back to normal.

Then for some strange reason, a record promoter was invited to sit in on one of the KFWB mystical music meetings. Although he couldn't recall who the promoter was, Bobby remembered the meeting well. "This guy left the meeting in a total state of shock. He kept saying to me, but they didn't listen to any of the records. It got so bad that the record, *I'm Blue* by the Ikettes was well on its way to being top 10 in the country but KFWB wasn't playing it because the jocks didn't like it. Every meeting I'd put the record in. The jocks would vote it out."

Finally, Bobby went to Chuck Blore. "I said, hey," Bobby recalled, "I thought the station was here to reflect the personal taste of its listeners. The records they buy we should be playing. That's what we're here for. And why do we allow the fuckin' jocks to vote against a record that's already number 10 in the country? Blore agreed and told me, Bobby if there's a record you know – not think – but know is a hit, put it on but tell me about it first."

Chuck Blore had a tight rope to walk with temperamental dj's – many with their own agendas – and an L.A. record industry determined to sell their product. But Bobby, at the time, had no idea the record meetings were often rigged.

"I could literally lay my head on the table and cry because of the situation and the power that I had," Bobby said. "I found out that people were getting paid $500 dollars if their record made our playlist, $100 dollars if you could get the fuckin' record to go in the meeting."

Bobby was aware of the payola scandal involving Alan Freed in New York but was as shocked as Inspector Louis Renault at Rick's in Casablanca that payola was going on right under his nose. Oh, Bobby would hang out with record guys and musicians and get his steak dinner and scotches paid for or get a box of albums for his "record hops" which never happened. But money passing behind his back to get records into "his" meeting and on the air furthered his rock 'n roll education.

One promotion man invited Bobby to coffee one day, asking that they be alone, and offered, free of charge, the services of a hooker being moved into an apartment across the street from where Bobby and his wife Carol lived in Hollywood. Bobby said, "I told the guy, you can buy her a fuckin' penthouse for all I care, but I'm not going to see her. People talk. Most of the little payola shit that I got was from Tamla/Motown. I would have played their records anyway. The first Marvin Gaye – *Pride and Joy* – I remember getting paid for, like a $100 bucks or some fuckin' thing."

Bobby wasn't in it for the money. He would have loved having some, but as he said repeatedly, "I was always broke. At that I was consistent." What Bobby loved was the music, the music people, the smoky bars, the booze and the roller coaster ride of being a number one disc jockey in Los Angeles. It was all part of the Wide Weird World of Bobby Dale – a wired world, an often tragic place where sex, drugs and rock 'n roll broke hearts and dashed dreams.

"I was always broke."

Bobby surveys his marijuana garden.

Bobby's best friend, Tommy LiPuma, also attended the Bobby Dale school of music appreciation.

20 The Walk of Fame

"The record promoters went to Tijuana and got a hundred uppers."

Aldo's restaurant and bar, next door to KFWB, was the watering hole for jocks, music promoters, hookers, musicians and artists. Bobby stopped in a lot. His Cutty Sark and water tall was only moments away after his shift ended at midnight. And most nights there would be a record promoter or two or more there to pick up the tab.

Bobby would most always be around the radio station and downstairs at Aldo's having coffee. B. Mitch Reed would stop in before his 6-9pm shift to prepare his show. Bobby said, "Mitch would order a double Chevas Regal on the rocks and then he'd pop a couple of green and white Dexedrine and wash it down with his scotch. I couldn't imagine doing that, man. I mean the drinking."

That was Bobby's firm and fast rule – no drinking while disc jockeying. But the pills were another matter.

"The record promoters went to Tijuana and got a hundred uppers, no questions asked. They'd bring 'em back and you could buy 'em from the guy. And, of course I did," Bobby said.

"Mitch didn't know what he was doing half the time," Bobby said. "In a nice way, man. I liked to sit in near the end of Mitch's show just before I went on. He had a gal engineer – her name was Patty and she was the only female engineer I ever worked with in radio. Mitch would be on the air talking a hundred miles an hour. I'd walk to where Patty was and ask does he do this a lot? She said, only for the three hours that he's on, man. But if you were in the booth with Mitch, it was chaos, and you know, it all came out on the air." Mitch was known as "The Fastest Tongue in the West" to which he would reply: "you're listening too slow."

In 1963 Mitch was headed back to his hometown to become one of "The Good Guys" at New York's WMCA. Bobby remembers his last show on KFWB. Mitch hauled in old 78's: Stan Kenton, June Christy, and the Woody Herman Band. "All records, I'm sure, that had a big influence on Mitch when he was younger," Bobby said. "But to play 'em on the number one Top 40 station in the country? I was there for the last hour and when I got on the air – I said I'm gonna play a long record while you help me get my audience back."

Chuck Blore and GM Bob Purcell had been forced out by then; Mitch considered it his good fortune to get out of the KFWB slow dissolve. And following his Jazzcapade finale, Jim Hawthorne, the new program director, told Mitch he didn't want him to work out his two-week notice. Bobby could understand why. Mitch was gone. But he'd be back.

By March of '65, Mitch was done in New York where he received a rousing sendoff before flying back to Los Angeles where he received a rousing welcome on his return to KFWB.

"You honor your friends while they're alive-not when they're dead."

After his Top 40 days had ended in the late '60's Mitch worked to help develop the counterculture FM Radio music explosion that became so hugely successful in Los Angeles and San Francisco.

Mitch died in Malibu, California of heart failure March 16, 1983. He was 56.

Bobby was invited to Mitch's funeral but declined. He did not like funerals, but it didn't mean he was indifferent. Mitch wasn't the first or the last of his friends who would be lost to drugs and alcohol. "I'm tellin' you man. I was the one who had the reputation for fuckin' up and for drugs and booze and for whatever else was around," Bobby told me. "I was always told you honor your friends while they're alive, not when they're dead." Bobby felt bad that his friend "the beamer" was gone.

Bobby agreed that in the early 60's, L.A. was the place to be. He said, "I loved to go there and why not? It's where everyone in the record business, tryin' to get their foot up in the movie business…they all were there."

Bobby met Phil Spector in 1962. Bobby said he didn't know much about Spector even though Bobby broke the Spector record, *To Know Him is to Love Him*, back in Fargo – the title taken from the tombstone of his father who committed suicide when Phil was 9-years old.

This first meeting was over another Spector record called *He's a Rebel*. The song was written by Gene Pitney and when Spector heard Pitney's demo of the song, he knew it was a hit and quit his A&R job at Liberty Records where he'd been working at the time. Spector had big plans for that song and his future career. But his old boss, Liberty Records produced a version of the Pitney song by Vikki Carr. Bobby said, "I couldn't believe it. Here was this gal trying to establish herself as a sort of nightclub chanteuse, a good music singer. But I couldn't figure out what the hell she was doing with that song."

Phil Spector produced a version of the song by The Crystals. Only they weren't The Crystals. The Crystals were in New York and in his rush to cover the Vikki Carr record Spector hired The Blossoms – Darlene Love, Famita James and Gracia Nitzschke to sing *He's a Rebel*.

Then the battle was joined

A young man named Tommy LiPuma, who'd talked his way out of Liberty's publishing department to become a promotion man, was assigned by Liberty to get the Vikki Carr record on the air…or else.

Spector hired a half dozen promotion men to hype his record and Bobby thought Spector had gone overboard in his scorched earth attack on the Vikki Carr version. Bobby began playing the Liberty version, in part to protect his new young friend, LiPuma, who was in danger of losing his job in this skirmish. Bobby always protected his friends.

That got Phil Spector's attention. He called Bobby to meet him for a drink. "I remember the first thing he said to me, man," Bobby recalled. We shook hands and he said I understand you read *War and Peace* twice? I said, yeah it was better than looking for a job." Phil Spector and Bobby Dale became friends.

Bobby was no longer on the music committee at KFWB but he did stand up and fight for The Crystals version of the record after meeting Spector. Bobby simply told the jocks there was not much doubt about which was the better record. The Vikki Carr record made the KFWB playlist securing LiPuma's job but Bobby refused to play it. "I bullied B. Mitch into not playing it," he said. "I didn't play it. And that took care of 6 to midnight at KFWB. You couldn't have that man. You had to have that record played in that time period."

He's a Rebel by The Crystals became the number one record in the country, and Phil Spector had Bobby Dale, in large part, to thank for it.

"One night I ran into Phil at Martoni's," Bobby said. "He was with two far out lookin' foxes from New York. They'd just flown into L.A. with Phil. We had a bite to eat and some drinks and ended up at Phil's house. Phil was playin' me a test pressing of *My Sweet Lord*. I remember telling him it sounded an awful lot like *One Fine Day* by The Chiffons. But meanwhile these two chicks are layin' on the floor makin' out, ya know? I said I'd better get home. I never had any weird things like that with Phil, but I did have an incredibly fun time with him."

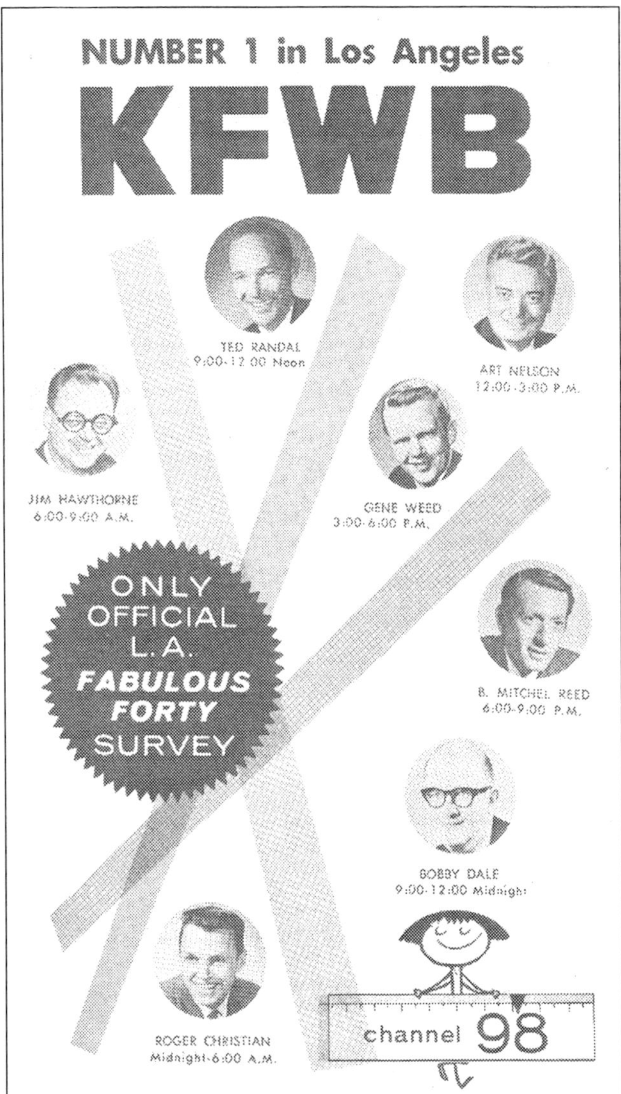

Phil and Bobby were the same age, both hitting their stride around the same time. Phil had several hits to his name after the Teddy Bears. He co-wrote *Spanish Harlem* recorded by Ben E. King, played the guitar solo on the Drifter's *On Broadway*, and produced *Corrina Corrina* by Ray Peterson in 1961. It hit number nine on the Billboard charts. In the fall of '61 Spector formed his own Philles Records and created what became known as The Wall of Sound – a full, pulsing, mono sound ideal for AM radio that Spector called his "Wagnerian approach to rock 'n roll."

Bobby said, "He was such an awe inspiring person in the record business. He was like some kind of god that lived up on this level. Everybody kinda had this image of Phil as an off the wall, funny guy, who was very talented at what he did. But there was more to him. He ended up the publisher of all the songs that were his: *Da Doo Run Run, Be My Baby*. They were all Mother Bertha Music which was the name of his mother. *You've Lost That Lovin' Feeling*...same thing. And you're talkin' about...just what that song has made in the way of money...ya know from publishing... from being used in movies like *Top Gun*. The fuckin' song sounds as incredible now as when it came out. And that was the one when Phil played it for me, I said: I can't hear it man. That's when he swore he'd never play another record for me."

"When I really heard the record I was riding to work one night and Dave Hull, who was on before me, was playing *You've Lost That Lovin' Feeling* and, I mean, it just blew me away. So when I got on the air that night…I must have played it 8 times between midnight and six in the morning. And after every newscast I'd come out with that (singing: You never close your eyes….). It gives me shivers now when I think of that record. But most of the stuff I did with Phil was just sittin' around talkin' about music, and song writers – people that always impressed me."

Bobby Dale had been impressed by the provocative and ground breaking talents of the black jazz and R&B pioneers, the likes of Jelly Roll Morton, Big Bill Broonzy, Charlie Parker, "Fats" Domino and Chuck Berry. He helped lead the way along with Alan Freed, Cleveland's Bill Randle, B. Mitchell Reed - and others - in exposing a new generation to the roots of rock 'n roll, the sheer cultural shock of it captivating black and white teenagers alike.

And despite his argument that it was rock radio's duty to play the records that reflected the tastes of its listeners, one of Bobby's greatest pleasures was being able to influence those tastes by giving history lessons, using his "golden ear" to recognize the potential hit records, then playing the hell out of them. He'd often delight in picking the flip sides of records being hyped by the record companies and their promoters. He could simply feel it and his reputation grew among the people who impressed him – the movers and shakers among the radio, music and record industry who were influenced by Bobby Dale.

"It gives me shivers now when I think of that record."

One of those people was Tommy LiPuma, the young man given the impossible task of promoting Vikki Carr's version of *He's a Rebel*, getting it played or losing his job. Bobby secured Tommy's friendship by saving that job and the two men became close, lifelong friends. In fact, near the end of Bobby Dale's life when I asked LiPuma why he liked Bobby Dale, he replied simply, "He is the best fucking guy I know." Bobby helped advance the career of his young friend, Tommy, who went on to accomplish great things in the music industry.

Tommy would become Chairman of Verve Records and is described on the Verve music web site as "one of the music industry's most innovative and uniquely creative forces for more than four decades."

"I was 26 when I moved out to L.A. …late '61, early '62," Tommy told me. "The impression Bobby made on me was so huge, that basically the guy changed my life. I was a promotion man when I first met him and he was on the 9 to midnight at KFWB. He orders two tall Cutty Sarks, and he literally guzzles this fucking thing down, picks up the next one and does the same thing. I wasn't keeping up two at a time, but I was keeping up. We got wasted and headed for his place and he puts some music on. We ended up putting *Don Juan in Hell* on and I was completely blown away. I'm just this fucking kid from Cleveland who was cutting hair just two years before that. I was a musician – a saxophone player – but it wasn't like I was all that worldly. But he was the first guy to open my brain. He was just mountains of information. It was like going to school, as far as I'm concerned, the best kind, ya know? No tests."

Tommy told me he became addicted to Bobby, would visit him on weekends when Bobby left for San Francisco. That was back when PSA Airlines charged $12 bucks for a one-way trip between L.A. and the Bay area. It was like a bus run with a flight every hour. It made it very easy for Bobby and Tommy to stay in touch.

In his tremendously successful career, LiPuma has worked with Diana Krall, Joe Sample, The Crusaders, Miles Davis and Doctor John. He produced the Natalie and Nat King Cole duet *Unforgettable* and the George Benson Album, *Breezin'*. He's been nominated for several Grammys and won two of them.

"I used to really admire Tommy's strength, man," Bobby said. "The guy was very strong with a great work ethic and he'd been great buddies with his engineer, Al Schmidt since, about 1962 – a great team. One time George Benson insisted on using the bass player that he had for his road band – not the recording band. This guy was no studio musician. Those guys you pay triple scale and you're lucky if you get 'em for that. They're that good. A studio musician got the job. Tommy knew what he was doin' even though I couldn't hear it."

"He'd come up with these things and you'd be in his spell."

When I asked Bobby if he had a best friend, he hedged. "Tommy would have been…but you know how things change in your goddamn life, man. You don't really see each other that much any more. I mean, if you wanna see LiPuma, you gotta go through an airport." Bobby hated flying and it was 20-years between flights, but he did get on a plane and flew to Connecticut to see his good friend. It was a profound gesture of friendship by Bobby who'd all his life kept most people he knew at a safe distance. Saying that Tommy "would have been" his best friend was as close as Bobby was ever going to get to saying he loved the guy.

Those early days in L.A. when Tommy was close by, were some of the happiest of Bobby's life.

"When we were deep into acid," Tommy recalled, "Bobby was, by then, doing the all night show at KRLA…he'd show up at my house in Studio City and stuff a pipe in my mouth. One day we'd be listening to *Afternoon of a Faun* by Debussy. The next day he'd come in with the new James Brown – *Sex Machine* – that we played 30 fucking times in a row. He'd come up with these things and you'd be in his spell…ya know? Nobody could throw music on a turntable like this guy, and mesmerize you. It was like going to school, everything from music to books. One minute he'd throw a Huxley book in front of me, the next minute a book on how the brain works. The bottom line is, I was very fortunate to have met this man because he helped me cut through the bullshit."

Tommy put his finger on why it is so difficult to describe on paper Bobby's sense of humor – his ability to reduce a person to tears with laughter – his natural gift for radio that captured an audience and "mesmerized" them.

"He was the absolute master of the one-liner, Tommy said. "I realized that some of the things that were hilarious were only hilarious if you were there. It was like something that happened then and there."

"At the Sunset Hyatt House where the rock stars hung out, somebody had given Bobby meth. In all the time that I'd ever known him, that's about as fucked up as I've ever seen him. He had, apparently, just been reading *Naked Lunch*, so he was completely gone on this meth tryin' to tell me how he felt and how all these lines that Burrows came up with – how much sense they made. Another day he shows up at my house. Someone had given me a placebo pill. I didn't know what the hell it was. It was this red gelatin-like, soft capsule. I pulled it out, had it in my hand and told Bobby somebody gave me this pill and I have no fuckin' idea what it is. Dale looks at it, picks it up with his index and thumb, looks at it, pops it in his mouth and says, well…we'll see. It could have been strychnine."

Bobby's more intense days of experimenting with drugs lay ahead. San Francisco and Los Angeles would vie for Bobby's talents as the Top 40 radio market began to undergo a seismic change in the mid to late 60's. In the process, it became increasingly difficult to keep track of the many times Bobby either quit or was fired.

As Bobby put it, "It's like everything else in my life…a repeat or a pattern…that every time, no matter how good and how short the hours…ya know…all the perks that went with it…somehow I could turn it into a job. And jobs were to be avoided at all costs."

Bobby's west coast odyssey began shortly after his support system – Bob Purcell and Chuck Blore – were forced out at KFWB.

21 On the Road Again

"Red Foxx was my hero."

In Top 40 radio, the not so subtle signs that you were about to lose your job were legend. The politics could be brutal after a change in administration. And when Jim Hawthorne took over after Chuck Blore moved on, Bobby Dale was in the crosshairs.

"Hawthorne was this kinda guy who'd get hung up on meaningless things," Bobby recalled. "In meetings, he would say, Bobby, you ran a so and so spot and you wrote it down as having run at 11:18. But he had checked the sound scriber, you know to find you were two or three minutes off on the log. I said maybe we all outta go to logging school. Gene Weed, who was sitting next to me and, of course, everybody else, laughed. And Hawthorne didn't have much choice…he hadda laugh too. But Gene Weed leaned over and said, Bobby believe me he's not gonna forget this shit. I said oh c'mon."

Bobby's next direct encounter was when Hawthorne called the station on a Sunday night while Bobby was on the air. "It just so happened that Crowell Collier was having a meeting in San Francisco of the heads of all three stations," Bobby recalled. "This was at the time – I believe it was the fall of '62 – the black guy, James Meredith was tryin' to get into the University of Mississippi."

Hawthorne wanted Bobby to remove

the songs *He's A Rebel* and *24 Hours From Tulsa* by Gene Pitney from the KFWB playlist. Bobby said, "Wait, excuse me, what are you talking' about, man? He said, well we wanna show that our sympathies are with this Meredith guy. And I said, maybe you outta go down there and march with him, man."

Hawthorne didn't see the humor, but later, recalling the incident, Bobby told me, "remember what Red Foxx said: I wouldn't join no group of marchers, man. He said, I'll take a cab and meet you there. Red Foxx was my hero. His classic line was: in my family color didn't matter. The only thing that mattered when the lights went out was who washed."

The final wake up call for Bobby came after all the KFWB jocks returned from a personal appearance, and according to Bobby, "stumbled all over each other to be the first to ask Hawthorne, hey what happened to Bobby? I didn't see Bobby at this thing. So, he wasn't there? Hawthorne calls me in the fuckin' office and instead of firing me, put me on the all night show. For my money, it was the end of my marriage and the end of my stay in L.A. If Blore had been there, I could have told him the fear of personal appearances is as real as anything I know. But it made no difference to Hawthorne. He was like a sergeant in the army…you're no different than anyone here. Get out there and entertain 'em."

And when I asked Bobby why he hated personal appearances so much, his reply, "'Cuz, I thought I looked funny and so did the teenagers."

Bobby's next order of business was ending his marriage to the girl he'd already broken up with five times. It took him some weeks to work up the courage.

His wife, Carol, told me she knew her marriage was in trouble. "We went through a period where he lied to me all the time," she said. "He was behaving as though he didn't want to be married. One day he didn't come home all night. He did that a lot. We had a baby – Johnny. I didn't phone after him. I don't like to do that. I've been in bars where guys signal the bartender and he says no he's not here. So I went into town with the baby next to me but I couldn't find him. When I got back home his car was there. I went in and there was a note on the table saying, wake me I want to talk to you. So, I woke him up. He came into the living room and we had a conversation that was pivotal, very sad and very satisfying. He said I don't want to be married anymore."

It was as simple as that. Bobby told Carol about the drink he'd had right after their wedding, with best man Charlie Boone; asking Charlie, "What have I done?" It dawned on Carol that what she'd sensed all along about their marriage was true and it was satisfying to her that Bobby had come clean and that their uncertain life together now had clarity.

Carol always loved Bobby. But their tumultuous relationship finally was over. Carol moved back to Minneapolis with baby John for whom Carol said, Bobby showed little affection.

22 The City

"There were looks of hate."

KEWB was located just across the Oakland Bay Bridge in Alameda County, tucked up against the estuary flowing to the San Francisco Bay in Jack London Square.

The area was named after Jack London, author of *Call of the Wild* and many other short stories, essays, and non-fiction essays, who was born in San Francisco and lived in Oakland, California.

London lived his early life as a hobo, an oyster pirate and a sailor. He attended Oakland High School, and wrote articles for the school newspaper. *Typhoon off the coast of Japan* was his first published work, an account of his sailing experiences.

In 1894, London wrote of his 30-day sentence for vagrancy in the Erie County, Pennsylvania penitentiary: "Man handling was merely one of the very minor unprintable horrors of the Erie County Pen (sp)."

It seemed fitting that Bobby Dale, in April of 1963, would be introduced to the hypnotic San Francisco Bay area in Jack London Square at a bar called The Pirates Den.

"Casey Kasem took me over to this horrible bar with dead roaches on the fuckin' floor. I mean a real drinker's bar where the entire staff of KEWB lived. It was like walking into a bar in Deadwood. All the jocks were there and I could feel the chill in the fuckin' air," Bobby recalled. "There were looks of hate. I had never had that experience before of walking into a new station, even though I knew some of the guys. I knew who they were. I didn't really know any of 'em."

The person he did know was the General Manager, John McRae who'd been top gun at KDWB in Minneapolis when Bobby was there. McRae was a hard drinking, bull of a man who had told his troops that his friend Bobby Dale was coming to town. Bobby said, "I'm sure John told them 'Bobby and I used to do a lot of drinking together back in the Twin Cities.' John always wanted to be one of the guys."

What Bobby didn't know was that McRae was the problem. He said, "From what I found out, McRae got drunk and started hitting on Hudson's wife at a party…a Christmas party. Bob Hudson – one of the KEWB jocks – who would kick the shit out of God if he thought he was wrong - went after fuckin' McRae, and damn near did him in."

"McRae fired Hudson, and that's whose place I took when I came to KEWB – Hudson's. I had never even heard of the guy, but when I heard him on the air, I said to him you're the one being fired? I mean he was the best jock I ever heard - the most creative. But, you know drink was a big problem with him. It was a shame, man, 'cuz the cat was supremely talented."

Crowell Collier's top management got wind of the McRae/Hudson dustup and called McRae on the carpet. McRae and the jocks hated each other and the chill at The Pirates Den was about: "Bobby, we've heard some incredible things about you and we'd like to know where you stand."

From picket line to the McRae Siegfried Line, Bobby had crossed into another high intensity zone, but aside from that first wobbly step, it was the beginning of the best chapter in his life. His patterns were the same but the bars were better.

"When I got up there," Bobby said, "It was insane. It was an entirely different game. I got together with Tom Donahue and every night we'd head to North Beach."

Donahue was the number one jock in San Francisco at KYA. Bobby Mitchell was a fellow jock and Donahue's partner in concert promotion, record promotion through their weekly Tempo Music sheet. They owned Autumn Records and as record producers worked with Sly Stone, Stone Ground and others with great success. Everything that would interest Bobby came in a single package orchestrated by Tom Donahue, a three-hundred pound plus "Big Daddy" whose motto was "Everything to excess." He was bigger than life.

Food, Drugs, Booze, Women, Life – you name it – Donahue devoured large chunks of it. Bobby loved being along for the ride.

North Beach was after hour's headquar-

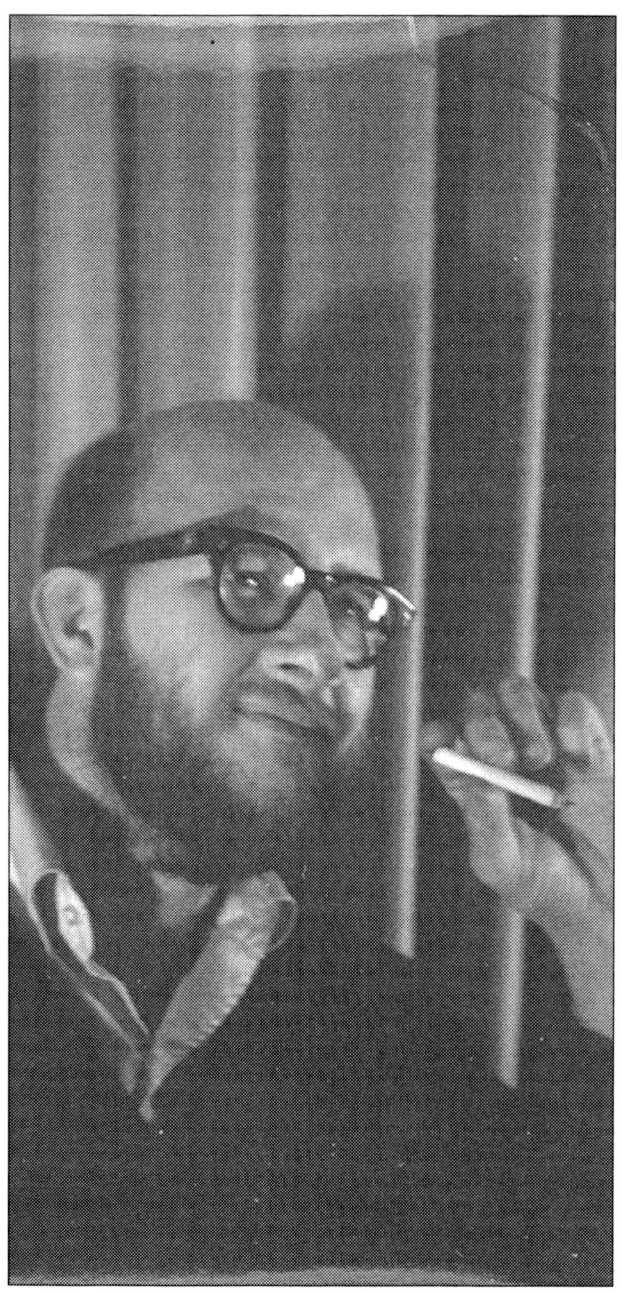

Tom Donahue told Bobby to grow a beard.

ters – a tacky bit of urban real estate concentrated in a two block stretch of Broadway near Columbus with The Condor - where Carol Doda's Topless Act made national headlines – on one end, to Basin Street West on the other, where the likes of Smokey Robinson, Otis Redding, Ike and Tina Turner, Lenny Bruce and Red Foxx appeared nightly. In between, the street was populated by every bit of sexual imagination possible, Triple X big screen movies and live nude antics of every description with hawkers at the front door stepping up to passing tourists to lure them inside for a two drink minimum and bare naked ladies, or men, or both.

Smack dab in the center of this sex carnival, at the intersection of Kearny and Broadway was Bobby Dale's favorite bar stool of all time – "The end stool at Enrico's next to the cigarette machine," Bobby said. "When my marriage ended, I'm sure Carol thought it was other women. Well it wasn't. I just like to hang out in bars, man. It was my life's ambition. And so for me…to come up here and go over to North Beach and to see all this in a two block area…I thought, my God man, I'll never have to leave."

Enrico's was the place to be. It was the hangout for politicians, musicians and poets – the "artsy type" the San Francisco Chronicle called them. When Enrico Banducci opened the place in 1958, it was the place to be and was within walking distance of the hungry i where Barbara Streisand, Woody Allen, Bill Cosby, Mort Saul and others got their start. A block away was The City Lights Book Store where Allen Ginsberg and Jack Kerouac hung out – Beat Generation writers whose Bohemia was North Beach.

Ananda Shorey wrote of San Francisco's so-called Beat Hangouts and of North Beach in particular: "North Beach, a gritty neighborhood where individuality rules, has long been a magnet for alienated, streetwise and rejected outsiders. In this destination for romantic visionaries, poems are still stuck to sidewalks with masking tape and buildings are painted shades of salmon, mustard and lemon meringue."

Next door to Enrico's was the legendary nightclub, Finocchio's, where men performed as famous women. Joe Finocchio got the idea in the late 30's while watching an inventive customer in his father's speakeasy imitate the legendary Sophie Tucker. Finocchio's was off limits to military personnel for a time but eventually became a favorite tourist spot and by the 60's when Bobby was next door, on the end stool at Enrico's, giant Greyhound busloads of folks from the Midwest, wearing mink stoles and superfluous baubles, would pull up to the curb and spill their passengers for a night of great fun. When Finocchio's closed in late '99, Lawrence Ferlinghetti – owner of City Lights Book Store simply said, "What a drag."

So, North Beach became Bobby's favorite place on earth. Not everyone knew his name, but the bartender did and that was all that mattered. And, in addition to live jazz, good food, great people watching and all the booze fit to drink, it was also the hangout for the record promoters, disc jockeys and visiting performers from Knob Hill – the lounges at the Mark Hopkins and Fairmont Hotels. Mel Torme, Vikki Carr and other nearby lounge acts would show up after their late shows for a nightcap at the round table by the front door reserved for visiting celebrity. Bill Cosby was a regular, always with a nod to Bobby. Dr. John would show up when he was in town and Tommy LiPuma, Bobby's close friend from L.A., who would fly up on weekends, was there. Just about anyone connected with Tommy's record label, Blue Thumb, which he co-founded, stopped by. Bobby would often feel inclined to relinquish his end bar stool to join the group, but mostly it was the group who joined Bobby around his end stool by the cigarette machine.

"I just like to hang out in bars- my life's ambition."

San Francisco also opened another escape route for Bobby. He said, "I was 33 before I ever smoked marijuana or any of the other shit that was going around. I didn't know shit about it. Never in L.A. and then to find out half the guys I worked with were smoking grass. I may have been 33 but I was naïve. I should have known. The first time I heard Ted Quillan was when he worked at KRLA. There was a thing in the paper…in the L.A.

Times…about this huge confiscation of marijuana. And Ted Quillan's on the air…9 to noon or whatever the hell it was…and he's on the air giving wind directions…and…THE BIG BURN IS SET TO GO AT 10:45 THIS MORNING…I RECOMMEND IT. They were burning like two tons of marijuana. At the time nobody I knew smoked marijuana. It came as a great shock."

"Tom Donahue liked to say he turned me onto grass…which wasn't true. It was a bartender from Enrico's by the name of Sandy… and his old lady, who I found out later, was a hooker. Sandy got off at two in the morning. We went to his place in one of those old flats in Pacific Heights, which is really a beautiful place.

They roll a couple of joints, and we lie around…we're smokin' and they're both lookin' at me, man. And I didn't feel anything…and then suddenly, of course, you started hearing weird things – like from far away suddenly sounded very close and when I talked I would stop because I realized I was listening to my own voice, man. It was a pretty incredible and intense experience."

Like with booze, which Bobby told me he fell in love with the first time he drank it, he realized with marijuana, too, he could, "alter my goddamn mood," as he put it. He liked it, but also realized it was an acquired taste. He bought his first "lid" of grass for $15 dollars in 1963 from a member of the improvisational group, The Committee. And Bobby welcomed another weapon to his mood altering arsenal.

"One night," Bobby recalled, "Tom Donahue and I go out ridin' in that big Cadillac and this big 400-pound man pulls out a joint. We smoked it and he said, hey, you wanna go to this bar where they have phones you can pick up and call some gal sitting over in booth eight? This is back in '63. He ordered a screwdriver. I had a gin and tonic. Suddenly Tom starts going through this paranoia bit…"Don't look"…"What?"… "That guy is a narc sitting three tables away." I said Jesus Tom, it can't be. Tom said we'll just pay the check and go. And I said wait a minute, don't you think it'd look better if we drank our drink. Tom turned me into a raving paranoid within five-minutes. So, he sits back down and now I'm really nervous. I whacked the gin and tonic down in record time. Tom did the same. And now we're worried that leaving too early would also look bad. And I said, well why don't we get on the phone and call somebody to help us…get us outta here, ya know? We didn't even know where we were."

In August of 1964 Bobby quit his job at KEWB. Shortly after, Donahue somehow talked Bobby into keeping him company on a trip to New York where he was working a deal with The Record of the Month Club. Bobby hated to fly but Donahue was a persuasive man – "Great movies," Bobby remembered Donahue telling him. "So we get on the flight at night and Tom goes to sleep immediately. He said you can have my drink, man. So when the stewardess came by I asked about the movies. She said oh, not at night – never at night."

Donahue did his business in New York and he and Bobby headed home and went directly to North Beach – this time to The Condor, a bar on the corner of Broadway and Columbus. This was the night that The City of San Francisco had warned the Condor and Carol Doda, "The Topless Queen of North Beach," that if she was lowered from the ceiling and appeared topless, she would be arrested and The Condor would be closed. It was a media event.

"I got there early and got my seat at the bar," Bobby said. "The bartender – Mack – is one of my best friends by now. And here comes Carol. She's a nervous wreck. Carol was a waitress when I first started hanging out there. She had this beautiful mouth, great legs and great ass."

"Mack and I headed upstairs to get a hit and when we came back down, they were all there. I mean…Channel 4, 7 and 2 were all there and everybody's waitin' to see if Carol's gonna…she's over there…oh, I'm so nervous…ooooh, this is just like the B-movie of all time. So Carol disappears and the band comes in to warm up. It's like…they didn't have a curtain or they would have done that, man. But down comes the piano and Carol had chickened out. She had this gauzy thing on top. Everybody was really depressed and totally pissed off. It was unbelievable."

The San Francisco newspaper columnist Herb Caen wrote: "The only reason they didn't close it down is she didn't have any breasts."

And now it became time for Bobby to move on. He climbed in his car – a Cadillac he'd bought with promotional albums given to him by record companies - and drove to Los Angeles. Bobby would sell those albums for a dollar apiece at local record stores to get that car. He loved it. It was his modest nod to payola history. Bobby never said why he suddenly quit. It could have been a number of factors but it was his pattern and that seemed to explain it to everyone who knew him.

Donahue may have played a role in Bobby's decision to head back south. While they were good friends Donahue could not resist taunting Bobby with KYA's dominant number one position in the San Francisco market. "I'd be driving over the Bay Bridge after my show ended on the way to North Beach," Bobby said, "and Donahue would play some record – B.B. King or something and say here's a song you'll never hear on that chicken 40 station" – referring to KEWB.

And Bobby, so far in his career, was in charge of the music and number one wherever he went. KEWB just didn't measure up.

So it was back to L.A. – still August of '64 – with no job, no plans and no prospects.

23 The City of Angels

"I wanted to goof around for awhile."

Bobby stayed with Tommy LiPuma at his little place in Laurel Canyon and went to work at KRLA in August of '64. Tommy was a friend of the station's program director, Reb Foster, who was an especially big fan of Bobby's and wanted Bobby back on the air in L.A. to help knock off KFWB.

"Reb Foster wanted me to do the all night show," Bobby said. "This was when they had Casey Kasem, Bob Hudson in the morning, Dave Hull, Reb Foster, Bob Eubanks. I mean they really had a strong recognition factor beyond belief. And Hudson…who I thought was the best morning jock I ever heard… Emperor Hudson, man."

Bobby knew that a strong morning man was the key to a successful Top 40 operation. And with the KRLA lineup, KFWB was beginning to feel the pressure. "KRLA was closing in a lot," Bobby said. "KFWB lasted a long time on their reputation and on the fact that people did want to work there, just to say you worked at KFWB."

Although the thought of competing against KFWB appealed to Bobby, the main reason he'd quit the KEWB job was because it was too much like a job and all his friends knew how he felt about work.

"I wanted to goof around for a while," Bobby said. "But Reb was really after me and I knew I couldn't say no. It was just when KRLA was really hittin' their stride."

Bobby began his new job on the Sunday night in 1964 when Bob Eubanks presented the Beatles for their first Los Angeles appearance at the Hollywood Bowl. And Bobby's time at KRLA, he admitted, was some of the most fun he'd had in radio.

Bob Hudson – the jock Bobby replaced in San Francisco - worked the all important morning slot at KRLA, only he was now calling himself "Emperor" Bob Hudson. "As a jock he was brash and egotistical," Bobby said. "I guess that's what you gotta be…because 'Baby you love the Emperor.' He'd been fired 32 times, but of all the people I've been around who I really thought had talent, he was incredible; not only voice wise, but ideas. The guy could really do anything."

Bobby felt good again about being with a winner. In Top 40 radio, you can actually feel it happening…or not. KEWB didn't have it. KRLA did. And if you're Bobby Dale, working the all night shift keeps you clear of management and permits opportunities to drift off the Top 40 record list and make some noise.

"It was a gas workin' there," Bobby said. "The station was really hot and I was havin' a ball playin' Rolling Stones shit. They had two albums of Stones in there. I started playin' a record the Stones had called *Off the Hook* – sittin' in my bedroom late last night…got into bed and turned out the light…it's off the hook. He'd called his chick and couldn't get through. Well, somebody from one of those expensive colleges that are prevalent in L.A. came out with all these Decca imports from France of Rolling Stone things. And one of them was *Little Red Rooster.* And on the other side was *Off the Hook.* I had petitions from people writing in tryin' to get them to release it. Tom Donahue even did a cover on it which wasn't very good."

Bobby's great pleasure was spotting a hit record and getting the listening audience in on it. KRLA turned him loose and it was music to their ears.

Bobby was having the time of his life, hanging out with his friend, Tommy LiPuma, working nights on a "hot" Top 40 station and his human nature being what it was…he quit and headed back to San Francisco.

Why? His friend Tommy said, "There were more interesting people up there than in L.A. He just gravitated toward Tom and Bob and the whole scene…Enrico's...and…. It was to the point where I was going up there every weekend."

And it was in San Francisco this time that one of the most interesting people he'd ever know walked into his life.

24 Teen Angel

Bobby settled back into San Francisco in 1965, got himself back on KEWB and reclaimed his bar stool at Enrico's. His job kept him in rent money and bar tabs. As before, KEWB was not the "hot" station, but Bobby was the greatest jock on the planet according to his number one fan who said, "So I'm punching around…it was an Isley Brothers song and I was very thrilled to hear it. Then the guy came in, gave the time and went into another R&B song. And I thought I really knew my music. Then he comes out and says…Bobby Dale and some one liner and I thought my god, did he really say that? I was hooked."

"Suddenly he was gone."

The fan was a 14-year-old girl named Norma Milanese – a Latina, Mexican beauty who'd just moved to San Francisco with her family from Levitt Town, Pennsylvania. She listened to WIBG back east - a rock station where Tom Donahue and Bobby Mitchell used to work. She hadn't yet dialed in Donahue or Mitchell – the number one guys. It was Bobby's music that got her attention. This all happened in 1963 – the first time Bobby worked at KEWB.

"Suddenly he was gone," Norma said. "It was killer. I didn't know if he quit or was fired. It was just really a drag. I was listening to KYA but not liking it. Then one day…it

was 1965…I'm pushin' the buttons again and I heard one song and knew it was him."

In fact, it was Bobby's first day back on the station. Norma telephoned the station, expecting a receptionist but Bobby answered the call and she told him how happy she was that he was back. "I hang up and remember telling my sister, Linda, Bobby Dale's back and I just talked to him. And I was all excited. Linda – who was 12 – had me call him again so she could say hello and Bobby was cracking up and laughing…talking to us. And then after he hung up he got on the air and said, I just talked to a couple of young girls in Richmond, Norma and Linda. They told me they were sisters but I don't know… they weren't fighting. Then he laughed his way into a song. At school the kids are sayin', I heard your name on the radio. I was always calling him, writing to him just about every day, all through high school. It was nice to have an adult you could talk to, who wouldn't look down on you and make you feel like a kid."

But Norma Milanese was no ordinary kid. After almost a year of phone calls and letter writing, she was peeved that she was not getting an invite. As she put it, "I was really pissed." Norma wanted to meet Bobby and she came up with a creative scheme to make it happen.

While Norma schemed, Bobby settled into a relationship with a young woman named

Norma was "hooked" on Bobby.

Judy Briscoe whom he had met in L.A. while he was still at KFWB. Judy was working a small record label and ran into Bobby at Aldo's next door to the station in Hollywood. They became friends.

Then Judy met someone whom she fell in love with and moved to San Francisco. but the love affair fizzled and Bobby ran into Judy again one night after returning to KEWB at – of all places – Enrico's.

Judy had always liked Bobby. She thought he was funny and smart and loved being turned onto the music and movies that Bobby loved so much. "I'd never seen *Treasure of Sierra Madre*, *Citizen Kane*…I mean I'd never heard of any of that stuff," Judy said. "Edgar Allen Poe stuff, Lenny Bruce, *Don Juan in Hell*…he really educated me on a lot of that stuff. We hung out with Tom and Raechel Donahue all the time. We just had fun together."

They had fun together and in 1965 moved in together as, what Judy described, "boyfriend and girlfriend."

All the while, Norma from Richmond had just turned 16 when she had a brainstorm. "I spent the night with my sister at a girlfriend's house," she said. "I got up early that morning and baked a cake. I think it was a chocolate cake. And all three of us got on a bus to Jack London Square in Oakland, went up to the radio station…and I had it timed so

Bobby and Judy- "Boyfriend and girlfriend."

"He was tall, good looking, dark hair."

that he'd just be getting off the air at ten."

Norma couldn't have been more excited. She loved this funny guy who was so great on the radio and I asked her, "Did you have an image in your head of what the guy looked like." She said, "He was tall, good looking, dark hair."

And she chuckled.

"They said Bobby's just getting off the air. If you want, you can go around the corner and watch him. It's a big glass booth and this was our first time of actually seeing him. Bobby was sittin' at the microphone and here is this big hulking guy with a bald head and a beard. And he's wearing sunglasses. I'm staring at him and my girlfriend who's standing beside me starts giggling and says 'Norma is that the guy you're going to marry?' Man, I just looked at her and said, 'yes it is."

Bobby walked up to the girls and Norma noticed he did something that she said, "struck me as something sweet."

"The first thing he does is smooth down the back of his hair, and he didn't have anything. I said, hi I'm Norma. He said, 'oh Norma' and held out his arms. I must've jumped three feet back. He started cracking up...really laughing."

One reason Norma brought her sister and girlfriend along was in case Bobby turned out to be "creepy," she said. "We left with Bobby, ran into a good looking record promotion man on the way out and sat with the two men while they ate breakfast. We had sodas."

"Bobby ended up taking us home to Richmond and he didn't drive real well, either. He reached into the back seat and gave us some records." And Bobby went on his way.

The next weekend Norma baked another cake for Bobby. This one was vanilla.

Then, Norma said, "It was writing every day and calling every day."

But Norma was not your typical teenage groupie. She was on a mission and Bobby was it.

Bobby was enjoying his return to San Francisco – not the job, but the people were more interesting than those leading the L.A. life. One of his favorites and a close friend was Abe Kesh, known as Voco (pronounced Vah'-Koh).

"He was a promotion man," Bobby said. "And the very first time I met him, man...I mean I remember it so vividly because we ultimately became such good friends and then his tragic end. Voco came over to KEWB – this was '63, the first time at the station. He wore a suit and a tie and he looked like...an Arab in a suit, man. He was really a different lookin' guy. But we hit it off immediately. I got to know Voco and his love of music... and his knowledge of music was even more than mine, which is hard to believe, at least for me."

Bobby, Tommy LiPuma and Voco formed a hard bond with music and laughter at its core. Tommy said, "Voco was like one of the funniest guys on two feet and on top of it he was like a musicologist. We'd go over to Abe's and sit at this table in front of this stereo system he had set up with cinder blocks and boards between them and all of the albums. And he had his speakers up. One minute you'd be listening to Edith Piaf. The next minute...he's the first guy who laid Otis Redding on me. He was just an unbelievable guy."

"And then it turned out," Tommy said..."it was sorta like the three musketeers – the three of us. And then what we'd do...on Saturday mornings we'd end up at Abe's house at about seven in the morning. We'd make it a point of being there by seven or maybe a little before seven because the cartoons would be on. We'd just stoke the pipe up and start watching all of the great Chuck Jones cartoons and just laugh our asses off for an hour or so.

BIG HITBOUNDS!

HAVE YOU SEEN YOUR MOTHER, BABY, STANDING IN THE SHADOWS?
Rolling Stones/London

THAT'S THE WAY IT'S GONNA BE
Lee Mallory/Valiant

LOVE'S GONE BAD
Chris Clark/V. I. P.

The popularity of records listed herein is the opinion of KFRC based on listener requests and retail sales in the Bay Area.

Win Your Chance To Join The Six Ten Men On A Fantastic Voyage To A Mysterious Island Loaded With Treasure In The . . . .

K-F-R-SEA HUNT

Send A Bunch Of Postcards With Your Name And Address On The Back To "SEA HUNT", KFRC, P. O. BOX 6146, SAN FRANCISCO. Then Listen For Your Name To Come Up On The Big Six Ten.

HAVE LUNCH WITH BOBBY DALE ON ISLAIS CREEK NOON-3

BIG 30

BOBBY DALE CROSSES NEW FRONTIERS EVERY DAY, NOON TILL THREE, ON THE BIG SIX TEN

BIG 30

BOBBY DALE . . .Noon Till Three On The Big Six Ten

San Francisco was always the city Bobby loved best, but he was tired of Top 40 radio.

Those were probably some of the best days in my life that I can remember; the most fun days. I never laughed more in my life. I never learned more in my life."

One of Tommy's favorite memories of Bobby was when he was working as a Liberty Records promotion man in 1962 while Bobby was still at KFWB. Tommy had already met Bobby over a couple of Cutty Sark and water talls, but as Tommy tells it, "Bobby didn't give shit who you were when it came to records. It was either good or not."

I was "working my ass off," as he put it, "trying to get in the door with the record *Papa-Oom-Mow-Mow* by the Rivingtons when I got a call asking excitedly if I'd been listening to KFWB. At that moment I wasn't. I turned it on. Well, Bobby started playing this record I was promoting. And what he did, he played it over and over and over again. He just kept playin' the fucking thing. This was on a Sunday night. By Monday, Music City – which was the record store at Vine and Sunset – they were goin nuts tryin' to find the record. It was an overnight hit in L.A. That was really the breaking point when we really started hanging out."

Tommy knew of Bobby's restlessness and trouble handling authority and said, "whenever it got to the point where he had to start going to meetings he didn't want to go to or dealing with people he didn't want to deal with, that's when he would make his move."

"When he did fire me I could have kissed him on the mouth."

And that in Tommy's mind was why Bobby made his move from L.A. to San Francisco and back so many times and why there were fewer and fewer stations where he wanted to work.

At one of his jobs working overnights and doing what he wanted to on the radio, he was asked to attend a meeting with a new program director. Bobby did not want to attend and told the General Manager to handle it.

These conflicts with management finally caught up with Bobby in 1965 when he was let go at KEWB – the first time in his career that he'd been fired.

Bobby had gotten tired of the rock radio grind and playing the same 40 records over and over, day after day. He signed a one-year contract at KFRC in San Francisco "We were all ex-top 40 jocks," Bobby said. "And before Bill Drake took it over it was like a KSFO without ratings. You didn't hear the Beatles. You heard a Beatle song by the Golden Strings or whatever. A lot of that KSFO did, but they had very strong personalities, man."

But Bill Drake – another successful Top 40 programmer – did take over KFRC to the objection of the entire on air staff. "They did not want to do it," Bobby said. "I couldn't afford to quit, but god I hated workin' there."

"Drake, himself was there one day. I was on in the afternoon, and he came in and I had just played Sinatra's *Strangers in the Night.* He said, 'Bobby I'm surprised you would play that.' And I said, 'Oh…well it's number one…why wait.' Certainly looked like a bona fide hit, Bill. But he said, 'yeah but in drive time I wouldn't think….' Man, I thought…I didn't say anything but how weird, of all the songs that you would not want me to play."

There were other scuffles over which Top 40 records to play and not to play. Which records would be on the restricted list and played at only certain times during the day.

There were rumors that payola was paid to KFRC people for getting records on the air. There was very little Bobby enjoyed about the Bill Drake experience.

Bobby did remember one thing he liked, "One of the great poster-like publicity photos I've ever seen was done there: KFRC PLAYS MORE MUSIC…and the jocks dressed in tuxedos and holding symphony instruments…kettle drums…bassoons. The weird thing is the people I worked for at that station were…they were great. Tom Rounds was one of the best I've ever…I just loved that guy, man. And when he did fire me I could have kissed him on the mouth. He said, 'Bobby I want you to know this is not coming down from Drake. This was my decision. You just don't sound like a happy jock'. I said you're goddamn right I'm not happy. But there was no doubt about it, I was not happy. And that's always been a problem. If I'm not happy you can tell it in two minutes."

It was the last Top 40 station Bobby would ever work. He put his bid in at KSFO – San Francisco's venerable middle of the road station – then took off for L.A. once again in search of a gig. There was nothing for him.

"I'm coming back to San Francisco in the fog," Bobby recalled. "God, it was horrible. I got home…I was living with Judy Briscoe then…and I went to bed at some ungodly hour, four or five in the morning. Judy gets back from lunch, woke me up and said 'you're to call Al Newman at KSFO'. I went over and it's Al Newman and his assistant Pete Scott who was a big, big fan. They said look, if we give you this show what are you gonna do? I looked at 'em and said, well, I thought I'd play some music, ya know? Bring some records in and play 'em. It is a radio station, after all. That was the clincher for 'em. They said great. The five other people they had interviewed had everything from tap dancing to Bar Mitzvahs on the air." Bobby didn't know it yet but he'd just landed the best job of his career.

25

The World's Greatest Radio Station

"You think you're high? I can barely see you down there."

KSFO is one of those legendary radio stations with a solid, storied past and now in the spring of 1967, while owned by Gene Autry's Golden West Broadcasters, Bobby Dale would join personalities like Al Collins, Jim Lang, Jack Carney, John Gilliland, Scott Beach and Dan Sorkin to bring sophisticated San Francisco listeners its very best all night show ever. The station was home for Giants Baseball, 49'er and U.C. Berkley football and San Francisco's best known sports broadcasting team of Russ Hodges and Lon Simmons. KSFO was described as a "skillful blend of personality music programs with a heavy emphasis on personality." The station was located at the apex of California Street on Knob Hill in the Fairmont Hotel. KYA was in The Mark Hopkins across the street. And a third radio station was close by in Stanford Court – another luxury hotel on Knob Hill. It was a class location for a high class radio station in one of the most beautiful cities in the world.

And it was his friend Voco that inspired Bobby shortly after taking the KSFO job. Voco – real name Abe Kesh – had taken a job on the air at KSAN, one of the free form California FM stations pioneered by Tom Donahue, Mitch Reed and others in the late 60's – the

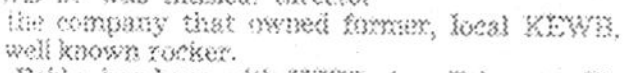

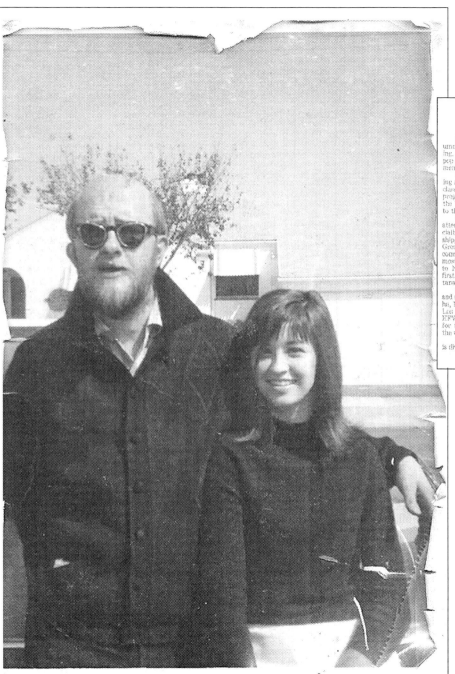

Meet Bobby Dale

(No. 72 in a series of TV-radio profiles.)

Bobby Dale is a favorite of many of this column's insomnious readers. From midnight 'til yawning, Bobby sits in a Radio KSFO booth dispensing pop records, no jazz, some rock, and a flow of comments.

Bobby's musical interests are catholic, embracing nearly everything, he says, from country through classical. He spends prodigious hours selecting and programming records that conform reasonably to the KSFO image. On KFRC, for a year, he adhered to the hard rock formula.

Born, Minneapolis, Minn., attended Minnesota U.; quit; specialized at a broadcasting school; shipped out on ore boats on the Great Lakes; mosyed around the country ("I am one of the foremost authorities on hitchhiking to New Orleans"), and got his first radio job at Glendive, Montana.

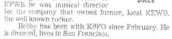

DALE

After that it was onward and upward to Fargo, N.D.; Omaha, Neb.; Minneapolis, Minn., and Los Angeles, Calif., where at KFWB he was musical director for the company that owned former, local KEWB, the well known rocker.

Bobby has been with KSFO since February. He is divorced, lives in San Francisco.

Tomorrow: Pat Paulsen.

Bobby's first meeting with Norma Milanese.

stations that would eventually suck the oxygen out of Top 40 radio.

"I listened to Voco's show on KSAN one Saturday night," Bobby said, "and it just blew me away, man. He played everything: jazz, pop, old…I mean really off the wall stuff but it was all good, and I thought, my god, why am I not doing all that. So then I started looking for songs I knew, that I liked. They were jazz, but they weren't the kind of jazz that scared people off. Not too many middle aged people I know sit around listening to Coltrane – which is probably just as well."

Bobby had just become his own program director.

"That was his prime time," his friend Tommy LiPuma said. "He was totally on his own. He was in this record library like a gold mine of things that he would find. God knows how many tabs of acid he would be taking. And he would just be able to fuckin' go on and on and nobody ever gave him any shit."

In San Francisco it was a time of change. A youth counter culture was being manifest in music, a free speech movement, the creation of "free form" FM radio and hallucinogenic drugs. Timothy Leary developed research at Harvard on LSD and other psychotropic drugs which showed great promise as psychiatric therapy. But when Leary migrated to San Francisco promoting the spiritual aspects of LSD and encouraging the "hippie" counterculture to "Turn on, Tune in, and Drop out," the challenge to the status quo began eroding any legitimate need for LSD.

Leary, in 1964, wrote of the psychedelic experience as "a new journey to realms of consciousness. It opens the mind, frees the nervous system of its ordinary patterns and structures." Enough was enough. In October, 1966 LSD was banned and all legal programs centered on scientific research of the drug, were shut down.

In the spring of 1965, Bobby was invited on an "acid trip" by a young woman named Deidre LaPort. "She was the gal," Bobby said, "Who was in a group Tom Donahue called Stone Ground…beautiful girl."

"She had two sugar cubes. I went to her apartment on Grand Avenue and we just kinda sat around and all I can remember is laughing at everything," Bobby recalled. "It didn't matter what the fuck was goin' on. It was an incredible thing. Deidre and I decided to walk down to the apartment where Tom Donahue had been living with my other good friend, Voco. When we stepped out on the sidewalk of Grand Avenue it was 3 in the morning and there was no one around. I mean, it was the most unbelievable scene. Everything looked like it was kinda cardboard…like a movie set. And Deidre and I are huddled together like Hänsel and Gretel. When we got down to Donahue's, here was Tom sitting on the couch and he had all these broken Amyl Nitrates around him and he was smokin' a joint. I didn't realize it…but to be around somebody who wasn't on acid…the first thing Tom said 'man am I high'. And Jesus, that just cracked me up 'cuz I thought…you think you're high, I can barely see you down there and you're 400 fuckin' pounds."

Bobby's penchant for self medicating had been satisfied by a new experience, of which he could not get enough.

Tom Donahue had gotten his "contact high" when Bobby and Deidre dropped in that first night of acid tripping along Grand Avenue. Now Bobby figured it was high time Donahue shared the experience.

"He didn't want to take it," Bobby said. "But eventually it was Tom and myself and a gal he was going with, Raechel – who he later married. That first time I took acid, Deidre kept telling me 'you don't have much of an ego…you've got nuthin' to worry about. I said, what do you mean? She said, if you were Tom Donahue, then I'd be worried."

Bobby tried to protect his friend Tom by advising him not to go outdoors. He was afraid that with someone like Tom with his incredibly strong personality, it could have been a "disaster," as Bobby put it.

In response, of course, Tom went outdoors where, with disheveled hair, and no shoes, engaged in a conversation with the landlord's daughter. Bobby said Tom loved it and by Saturday night Tom thinks he's found the answer to everything. I knew what he meant."

"Tom thinks he's found the answer to everything."

Raechel Donahue was an especially big fan of Bobby's and meeting him made a strong first impression. "He was on his selected barstool at the legendary Enrico's," she said. "He was chatting amiably with Lucky, also known as Lucky the Killer, and not because of his good looks. Lucky wasn't beefy like a bouncer, but he was tall and he looked like evil incarnate, even when he smiled. Whatever Bobby had just said to him made the Killer burst into a joyous, delighted and totally uncharacteristic laugh."

"Tom and Bobby had a traditional greeting," she said. "Tom would say, 'how are ya man'? And Bobby would say, 'totally depressed', his head and voice dropping low at the last syllable. 'Good, then you're happy, right man?', and Dale would bobble his head with a hint of a snicker. 'Yeah, man'. There was nothing Bobby liked more than a really cloudy, gloomy, rainy day. It was lucky he ended up in San Francisco."

That was Bobby in a nutshell – happy being unhappy. It was his unique character that played so well on the radio as he weaved his all night musical web, as though we were all back at his place listening and getting loaded.

When Bobby began his run at KSFO, it was obvious from the start that he was making a big impression on other jocks. They would call Elma Greer who Bobby called "a sweetheart of a music librarian" and she would leave a note telling him there'd been requests for his playlist. Bobby, of course, had no playlist.

Bobby said, "Jack Carney called me at home one day: Bobby, Jack here. I said, yes Jack what can I…he said you played a song at about 12:30 this morning and it was just a killer. And I said do you know…No, I don't know the name of it…the guys name is Richie…I said Richie Havens. That must have been *I Can't Make it Anymore.* He said that's it man, the greatest fuckin' song I ever heard." (And then Bobby sang a few bars – "I get too low without a reason. You say it's the moon or the season. But somethin' sure is wrong… and I just can't make it anymore.") "That was the first record I ever heard by that guy - On Verve Forecast."

Not all the jocks were so easily educated. Don Sherwood, the morning man, was in charge of programming and wanted Bobby's help picking the music. Sherwood had gotten feedback from listeners who caught Bobby's show telling him how much they loved the music.

"I recommended a record to Don because I knew he liked country music," Bobby said. "Don said, what is that? And I said it's a record by Don Gibson called *Sea of Heartbreak.* When I brought that record to him, I never questioned the fact that he might NOT like it. And I'm in the back…and the record's playing on the air…and suddenly he comes in… 'TAKE IT OFF.' I went to him and said what happened. He said, 'Too many do wahs in there, man'. I just sorta washed my hands of the whole thing."

Bobby just stuck to his all night gig and tried to keep a respectful distance from anyone even remotely associated with management, while continuing to educate not only the KSFO jocks, but jocks at other radio stations. Some knew Bobby or knew of him, just by listening to his show.

One of them was Johnny Hayes, a 23 year old young man from Macon, Georgia, brought to KYA by Bill Drake and warned to stay clear of Bob Mitchell and "Big Daddy" Tom Donohue. Hayes wanted to know why. "These are different kind of people from you and me," Johnny recalls Drake telling him.

"These are strange people. These people are on a different wave length. Well, within a couple of weeks, I was completely under the control of Mitchell and Donahue. These were the most incredibly colorful, fantastic and dynamic people I'd ever met. Donahue felt I needed experiences in life. I just was a kid. And he used to take me places to meet strange and unusual people."

One night, Donahue, who worked the 6 to 10pm shift called Johnny at home where he was napping before taking on another all night shift at KYA. Donahue told him to get dressed,

"He was a great mystery."

meet him at the station, that he wanted Johnny to meet one of the most unusual characters that ever walked the earth. Donahue told Hayes this was the man's first day in San Francisco and they were meeting at The Off Broadway in North Beach.

"Donahue and I walked into the bar," Johnny remembered. "And there was this strange looking tall guy with a bald head wearing all black, smoking Kool Regulars and drinking gin. It was Bobby Dale and we started a friendship that was closer than close for over 25 years. He was a great mystery, and the closer you got to him the more mysterious he was, because he revealed so little of his inner thinking and inner workings."

"I spent many, many nights with Bobby at KSFO." Johnny said. "He would have the engineer segue records and he would take me into the music director's office and play records for me. He was running two shows simultaneously."

When I tracked down Johnny Hayes and told him I was working hard to tell "The Bobby Dale Story", Johnny said, "The thing that's going to be difficult for you to tell is the fact that drugs played a tremendous role in his life. However, he never got fucked up and out of control. I believe that the drugs enhanced his thinking abilities and I think he was able to probe deeper into the subconscious and into the many hundreds of books he had read and the things he had remembered from those books. And he would get high and listen to music and I believe he got more deeply into the music than many people. I would sit there on the sofa and look at him and you could tell that he was virtually at the session in which the record had been made."

While it's true Bobby never got 'out of control' on drugs, he would and did get 'out of it'. And one night it nearly cost him his job.

"I wasn't drunk," Bobby said. "I just had no sleep. I never drank on the air except near the end when I didn't give a shit anymore. I was not maybe, addicted to amphetamines, but I always felt I needed them – pop an upper before the show, fuel it with coffee and then run out into the lobby of the Fairmont Hotel and see if you could get lucky. I always had my little matchbox with 10 different kinds of pills in it. One morning I left it in the booth when Sherwood came in. I came back in when a record was playing and said 'Don, I left something. He said go ahead and grabbed my matchbox and said this is my show for tomorrow. You get into those crutch situations and that's the way I am. I was the same way with acid. I'd be taking it like an upper, ya know? And bouncing off…gee those colors are great tonight. This is the way all shows should sound and look. The biggest problem I had was trying to sleep."

Bobby's lack of sleep caught up with him right after the Superbowl of 1968. Bobby had been up for days and sometime during his show he called a young woman named Norma Milanese – the very same Norma who'd baked a chocolate cake for Bobby and had taken it to him on a bus to Jack London Square back in '63 when she was a mere 14 years old. He invited her down to sit in during his show.

Bobby said, "Once Norma met me that was it, man. I was the one. She didn't say anything at the time, but how the hell she even knew to show up at KSFO that Sunday night when I passed out on the air."

While still living at home in Richmond, Norma and her sister and girlfriend would cook up elaborate stories for remaining away overnight. Norma would show up at the Fairmont Hotel and sit in with Bobby at KSFO.

"He never invited me. He never touched me," Norma said. "Nothing's happening. He never laid a hand on me. I'm getting really frustrated. And I'm telling my sister, I'm getting laid tonight. I was so tired of not getting any response from Bobby that I just said screw it. I've been saving myself for three years and counting down the days on every single letter I sent him. It never dawned on me that I was jailbait."

"So we go to Carmel," Norma recalls. "It was Friday night and we're on the beach. A couple of guys came along...and I'm... nope...it ain't gonna happen, Norma. Until this one dude came over with this big jug of wine, and holy smokes...unbelievably beautiful kid...about 26 years old. It was great. Right there on the beach with the full moon. Unreal. But when I got back to my room, the first thing I said to my sister was...I think I'm pregnant."

It turned out Norma was pregnant, three days short of her 18th birthday, living in an Italian, Mexican, Catholic family with four Italian brothers.

Norma ended up the center of attention at the Haight-Ashbury Free Clinic, escorted to a room, asked to undress from the waist down and get up on the table. There were guys in the room littering the floor. Norma protested to no avail and the guys got up to watch Norma's first pelvic.

"It was so humiliating," she said. "But I knew no one else to turn to.

After tests, it was determined that Norma was, indeed, pregnant and was told she'd need two psychiatrists to sign off before any abortion could be performed.

Norma described her one-sided three year love affair with Bobby and how she'd come to be in this pickle to the head of the Abortion

League in San Francisco who told her he could not help her. He said he'd been performing too many abortions and "they" were watching his every move.

But he suggested Japan or Mexico as an option for her.

Norma said, "I can't stay out past midnight." And she began to cry. The doctor finally relented. Norma told her parents she'd be babysitting for friends and staying at their house for a few days and headed for Children's Hospital in San Francisco where she was admitted the night before the abortion was to be performed. She called Bobby around 5 in the morning and told him her story. "He said, I wish it had been me," Norma recalls. "And damn…did that hurt. I'd been waiting three years and then getting so confused…and then blowing it. And then finding out…that's when he told me, 'hey I couldn't touch you'. You're jail bait."

The next day Norma had her abortion.

Shortly after, Norma moved away from home and got mixed up with a bunch of hippies who moved in with her. They sponged off her, crowded her and used her car. "I was just depressed and broke," she said. "So finally I threw everybody out of the house and called Bobby one night. It was around Christmastime, 1967 and I just started crying on the phone."

Bobby told her to come to KSFO and she began her Friday night ritual again. "And then," she said, "right after the Superbowl of '68, Bobby called ME for the first time and says why don't you come on down? And I thought, holy smokes, this is what I've been waiting for my whole life. So I go down to the station and Bobby looked bombed. He was walking down the hallway…going from one side to the other…back and forth…back and forth."

Bobby told Norma he'd been up for three days, taking uppers and watching football. "Bobby was really, really tired," she said.

"He was drinking coffee and drinking sugar water. He must have taken 6 Desbutals – part valium, part upper."

The net effect was the valium took hold. The upper did not.

Bobby remembers some of that night. "The phone is ringing off the hook," he said, "and it's young people calling from Berkley saying we're taping your show and it's incredible. How much have you had to drink? I said I had not anything to drink. And I hadn't. Of course now I get on the air and I'm arguing with people – I'm not drunk, I talk funny, that's all. By the time I did the three o'clock news…I was sitting there with only one story…I read it…it was about Arnold Palmer shot a 69 today in the Los Angeles Open…and I said that's interesting. And the engineer, Jerry Thompson, cut me off and put a record on. He called the relief man, Dick McGarvin who lived about two or three blocks away, and he came over."

"I'm not drunk, I talk funny, that's all."

And the weirdest thing," Bobby said, "was Norma was there. At this time I barely knew Norma."

In his sleep deprived condition Bobby had apparently forgotten he'd invited Norma to join him that night. And that, as it turned out, was the weird part.

Thompson asked Norma if she could take Bobby home. Thompson helped Norma guide Bobby down the back staircase and out onto California Street which tilts at about a 45 degree angle…and it's raining.

Norma said, "The first thing Bobby does is go slipping and sliding. Just vroom…his feet went out from under him and the glasses got broken."

Jerry and Norma got Bobby into her two tone blue '58 Chevy and now Bobby has become all Norma's problem – a giant of a man to be taken up a flight of apartment stairs by a five-foot-four-inch, 92-pound girl.

Norma pulled her car right up to her front door and somehow got Bobby into her apartment, took off his pants, shoes and shirt and aimed him at the bed and let him fall. He passed out. Norma sat in a chair all night watching him, then decided to press his pants, and wash his socks so that all his clothes were ready in the morning.

When Bobby opened his bloodshot eyes, he saw Norma in the chair and asked, "Did I? Did we…?

Norma told him he'd just been sleeping and Bobby appeared grateful for that.

Bobby said, "Normi showed up at the station that night. I wasn't having anything to do with her. And suddenly I wake up, ya know, from this horrible nightmare and I'm in her bed. I had no idea how the hell I got there. The only thing I remember is that Arnold Palmer shot a 69 in the L.A.…and that was the only story I had with me when I went to do the 3 o'clock news."

Bobby headed straight for KSFO to explain what happened. "I knew I was in big trouble," he said. "And the first thing Al Newman said was 'you know we were considering you for the 8 to midnight shift, but after listening to this tape…. I said, Al I can't convince you I'm sure, but believe me I hadn't had even a drop. He said, Bobby what happened. I said I didn't get any sleep. I got the 8 to midnight show."

Bobby called Norma later in the day to tell her he not only had saved his job but had gotten a better shift and that he'd told his girlfriend Judy Briscoe that he'd spent the night at her place, and that Judy had thrown him out, believing that they'd slept together.

Norma told Bobby he could stay at her place." He came over with a whole armload of clothes and we started living together," she said. "Just like that, my wish came true."

The Desbutal incident somehow got whispered about, and when rock journalist Ben Fong-Torres set up an interview with Bobby for his book *The Hits Just Keep on Coming*, he said, "Before we start can I ask you a question?" Bobby recalls. "I said sure. He said there's a rumor that was pretty strong in the industry that you were taken out of the booth and put on a stretcher at KSFO and taken to the hospital. I said, no fuckin' way…they left me in the lobby."

Ben Fong-Torres was fascinated with Bobby Dale. In April, 1982 he wrote a story for the San Francisco Examiner titled, *The Many Faces of Hessman.*

The piece was essentially about Howard Hessman's San Francisco roots, his early life as a denizen of North Beach in the 1960's, his drug use and his political protests as a member of The Committee – a comedy improve group. Hessman's talent as an actor took him to L.A. and landed him a starring role in the comedy series, WKRP in Cincinnati, as Dr. Johnny Fever – "the only pothead in prime time," Hessman was fond of saying.

Hessman admitted dealing in pot during the 60's when it sold for $15 dollars an ounce. And although Bobby never mentioned a name, he did say he bought his very first "lid" from a member of The Committee. Coincidence? Perhaps.

Hessman was a friend of Tom Donahue and for a time worked as a jock Saturdays on KMPX – the ground breaking San Francisco "underground" FM station. Hessman told Fong-Torres that his friend Bobby Dale was one of the models from the 60's that helped mold his character, Johnny Fever, on WKRP in Cincinnati: "Whatever he's doing, he wants to do it well. But he doesn't seek to do a lot."

"The look, Hessman was quoted as saying, "is inexpensive. It's all pretty much one color. I mean, you can't get too mixed up in the dark if all your socks are white."

Fong-Torres wrote: "The description fits Bobby Dale pretty well. Told he was a fashion inspiration for Johnny Fever, Dale was delighted. "Great!" he said. "Can I sue?"

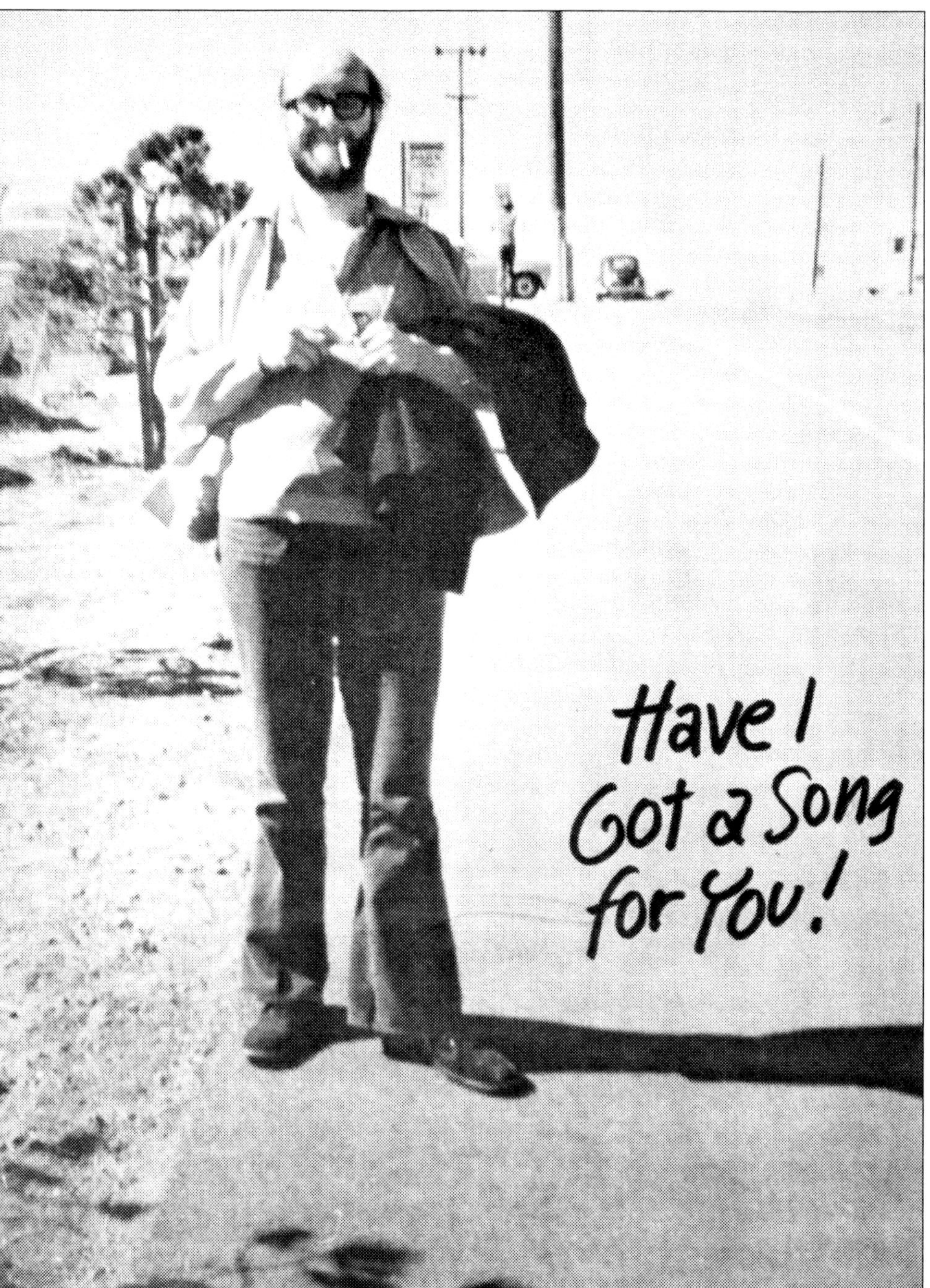

KSFO poster for which Bobby joked he only had to pay $29.95.

26

The Rock Revolution

" 'Progressive Rock' turns 'Top 40' on its ear."

"Big Daddy" Tom Donahue – then unemployed – wrote a Rolling Stone Magazine article in 1967 titled "AM Radio is Dead and its Rotting Corpse is Stinking up the Airwaves," an indictment of the Top 40 format.

In March of '67, Donahue took over KMPX, a foreign language FM station and produced America's first "progressive rock" or "free form" radio station, playing album oriented bands, many of them from San Francisco: Big Brother and the Holding Company featuring Janis Joplin, The Warthogs, a band that eventually became known as The Grateful Dead, Quicksilver Messenger Service, Creedence Clearwater Revival, We Five and so many others that kept The Avalon and Fillmore Auditoriums packed with teenagers and young adults throughout the late 60's.

Donahue, himself, worked the 8 to midnight shift and hired on Abe Kesh, Edward Bear, Bob McClay – the voices of KMPX - and "chick engineers" to run the boards and play the records. Donahue was a man who surrounded himself with beautiful young women. His wife, Raechel said the "chicks" were hired because Tom liked looking at their legs and because they worked for less money. One of the first "chicks" to be hired was Dusty Street who fit that bill and had been in the Bobby Dale orbit on and off since the Los Angeles Top 40 days. She learned her music lessons well and went on to greater fame with "Big Daddy," and even now broadcasts daily on Sirius Satellite Radio from The Rock and Roll Hall of Fame in Cleveland, playing progressive rock music at age 61.

In late 1967, KMPX owner Leon Crosby acquired KPPC Radio in Los Angeles. Donahue programmed both stations but then his project went south. He was replaced as program director and the staffs of both radio stations formed a union and went on strike with the support of the musicians whose music was the beating heart of this new kind of radio.

The strike lasted eight weeks and KMPX, now limping along with none of its original staff and few advertisers, attempted to continue its "progressive rock" format but was now facing an even greater threat to its continued existence. Tom Donahue had set up shop at KSAN-FM, 94.9 on the dial, a Metromedia station that had been broadcasting classical music. He set a new cast of on-air voices including that of Dusty Street, and his own wife Raechel.

Donahue transformed KSAN into "The Jive 95" – "The hippest station in the universe," according to Frank Zappa. It was a dynamic and innovative experiment that not only attracted an audience but with a force that Top 40 radio never did. But its success also set the plate for album oriented rock radio in every market in the country. FM radio, which had been largely ignored until the San Francisco experiment, was suddenly the toast of the town.

"Progressive rock" largely meant heavy metal, psychedelic, folk, blues but always with rock music at its core. The disc jockeys were given free reign within the format to play the albums they liked and talk about the raw-nerve social issues so prevalent in the late 60's – especially in San Francisco. At first, the San Francisco area rock bands were a centerpiece at KMPX and KSAN but the format embraced attempts by the rock music industry to get more album play, to get beyond Top 40. Albums like Sgt. Peppers Lonely Hearts Club Band which contained no single Top 40 hit, became a hit itself and got all the airplay it needed.

The length of a record in the salad days of Top 40 radio was a factor in the frequency of its airplay; short records, more commercials and whiz bang. Fats Domino records, for instance, ran around two minutes in length, and although they were great they got more airplay because they were short. By the mid 60's, Top 40 radio audiences were getting older, the various formats were getting stale, and subtle changes were already underway.

All night jocks, like Bobby Dale, were already aware of longer album cuts by hit artists and began playing them to great effect. The audience loved them and those lonely 6-hour all night shifts became easier to bear. Recall, Bobby's advice to Bill Balance; "play the 12-minute Creedence cut instead of the 2-minute cut."

By the time Donahue, his "chicks" and "voices" hit the ground running, the rock music market was awash in hit albums from Dylan to the Beatles, experimental album tracks and what were called "turntable hits" – album cuts that were heavily requested by listeners but never sold. It was a free form, mixed bag that opened a Pandora's Box of ideas applied in different ways at FM radio stations throughout the country. Rock and Roll was here to stay but Top 40 radio was not.

Raechel Donahue, wife of "Big Daddy" Donahue.

Of Bobby Dale, Ed Bear – one of Donahue's voices – wrote in a note to Norma, "Did you know that Bobby Dale was an elf who grew tall so people wouldn't recognize him as an elf? Bad people will capture elves and do terrible things to them to try to get a location on a pot of gold. Bobby did what he could to spread laughter so people wouldn't fight and wouldn't notice he was an elf. You know, if you're laughing, it's hard to hit someone, right?"

Those who knew him were always trying to get a handle on him and Ed Bear's description was among the most creative.

Over at KSFO, Bobby was having some of his best days programming his own brand of "free form radio" with jazz, blues, folk, country, classical and even rock 'n roll music. "After 3am the music got a little more jazz – off the wall type jazz things, but very listenable," Bobby said. "I never tried to make my show for only certain people. I mean I always played a lot of popular music, but it always had a jazzy feel to it."

But would Bobby also throw in a rock 'n roll record to show his versatility? "Oh, absolutely," he said. "I would have played *Linda Lu* by Ray Sharpe every fuckin' night. I loved the record."

These were the good old days for Bobby. He had a great job with no interference from management, a beautiful young girlfriend who became his sidekick. Norma organized his music, answered his fan mail, and spent countless hours attending classes in the Wide Weird World of Bobby Dale.

"He was so funny," she said. "He had all these incredible one liners, and he started turning me onto Lenny Bruce records and Lord Buckley…a lot of spoken word type things. He was just sort of a mixture of all this stuff. He was Thurber, Charles Schultz and Max Shulman."

Bobby first picked up on Lenny Bruce while working in Fargo. He said, "A record promoter said to me: Listen to this: and this voice said, Helen Hayes is a fink...I'm the real Anastasia. One time Bob Krasnow with Blue Thumb asked me if I'd be interested in hearing all the Lenny Bruce tapes. I took them home and Tommy had it set up so I could listen at night with headphones on. You look in the den and there's some fuckin' bald headed guy with ear phones on...laughing. He had some funny bits, like the Indians were talkin'. If you let one white person in this neighborhood, before you know it the whole neighborhood's gonna be white. Not only that but they go to the bathroom in the house."

Bobby and Norma would spend late nights getting high and listening to music. He would wrap Norma in a blanket on the couch and make love to her with his record collection and turntable. After a time Norma even began taking on some of Bobby's mannerisms and patterns of speech and inflection. They became two peas in a pod.

On the air, Norma became Carmelita – a name Bobby gave to her because, "I just didn't think she looked like a Norma. I called her The Rose of Richmond."

Norma/Carmelita could often be heard in the background at KSFO but she was never on the microphone. Bobby's only other on-air player was Bobby. He used to talk with himself – make a stupid comment and call himself stupid. He'd have conversations with himself and often Norma played a foil in his ramblings but she was never on the air.

Norma's job was as Bobby's ersatz personal manager – keeping him safe and loving him. Bobby Dale was her life.

One early morning after smoking hashish in the announce booth Norma heard the buzzer go off at KSFO's front door to the lobby in the Fairmont Hotel. There were uniformed police officers standing on the other side of the plate glass with weapons drawn. They told Norma through the intercom there was a search underway for a criminal last spotted in the hotel and they needed to enter the station to confirm the man was not on the premises.

High on hash and panicked, Norma nonetheless calmly told the officers to come in but stay clear of the announce booth when the red light was on because they were in the middle of a broadcast. Norma then rushed to the booth, told Bobby the story and to keep the red light on. She then escorted the cops around the station. They were satisfied no criminals were lurking and went on their way. Whew!

Bobby was enjoying his life and it showed on his radio program. His fan mail reflected his better moods: "Bobby, just a note of thanks. It's always the best moments on radio listening to your shows," wrote John Dombrink. And Lenny Baymon of Oakland: "Okay, so you were gassed tonight. So what. In my humble opinion, you are still the best."

And the truth of it was when Bobby was happy he was the best. Ron Lyons, one of Bobby's friends and colleagues from KEWB in 1964 was drawn to Bobby from the first day when he walked into KEWB wearing a Sy Devore suit, palming his cigarette with the lit end toward his hand. "I thought it was very cool," he said. "As a talent, he was amazing. I used to listen to Bobby every day on the way to work and marvel at his ability to be exactly like he was in person. The best word I can use to describe him was gentle."

Being "gassed" on the air was Bobby's trademark. He would joke about dashing across the Fairmont lobby to the Tonga Room for exotic drinks while his engineer played some tunes. But the truth was Bobby never drank alcohol while working. He knew where it could lead.

His references to booze, loose women and lack of money, as in "I scarcely made enough money to go out to the local 20 acres ranch" in Glendive, Montana was part of his act and part of his life. He would converse with himself on the air: "How long y'been on the air, kid...ya mean tonight...or since my showbiz career burst forth like a supernova in Glendive, Montana January 13, 1956?" Bobby's near photographic memory combined with his bootleg heroes – W.C. Fields, Lord Buckley, Lenny Bruce and Homer Simpson – his natural gift for humor and music made for some exquisitely entertaining radio moments. But, you had to be there.

"The best word I can use to describe him was...gentle."

Because Bobby did his own newscasts at the top of every hour on his all night show, you could always tell when the acid was flowing freely. There'd be laughter...waves of laughter, and off the wall stories if he could find them. He would talk his thoughts out loud to himself during the newscast: "You had one good happy story and now you can't find it."

"I had a story about Howard Hughes and talked about how he wouldn't answer any of my letters." Another reference to his shaky financial condition.

"I used to run a thing called THE BOBBY DALE BENEFIT which would be coming up any time...as soon as we could find some people with money." That little bite at humor got Bobby called into the front office. Bobby related the story of being called on the carpet by the program director, Al Newman – the man that hired him. "He said, now I know that's just part of your schtick there, Dale. He said we've had a few people call and wonder why you can't pay this man enough to live on so he doesn't have to do benefits. Of course, I wasn't gonna do a Bobby Dale Benefit. That would require me showing up somewhere."

His music librarian, Elma Greer, who loved Bobby and thought he was great on the air, would describe him as too esoteric "for Don (Sherwood) and his truck drivers and longshoremen" who tuned in as Bobby slid toward sunrise at the end of his all night shift. Elma even offered to program the music in the last hour of his show. "You should be very commercial," she wrote in a memo.

It was a gentle suggestion and an offer of assistance. For a man who had no confidence with women, he certainly had protection from a number of them. They wanted him to be happy and succeed. But Bobby's depressive tendencies and prolonged periods of amphetamine use began taking their toll.

"Tom Donahue would swear up and down that he heard me one night say...where the fuck did I put that thing," Bobby recalled. "That I not only said it on the air, but when I realized the mike was open, I said, 'Oh fuck I'm really screwed. But I know that never happened, because regardless of the time, there would be repercussions."

But maybe not. It was a well known fact that radio honchos he worked for may have wanted to fire Bobby from time to time but didn't because either he was getting high ratings or because they loved him and wanted him around.

When Bobby told me about Donahue hearing him say "fuck" on the air one late night, I tended to agree that it couldn't have happened, until I had a chat with Dan Hicks, a talented musician that caught Bobby's attention with a group called Dan Hicks and his Hot Licks. Bobby would play Hicks' album a lot.

"He indulgd in one drug and another most of the time."

Dan got to know Bobby. He'd sit in at KSFO on occasion and watch Bobby perform his unorthodox disc jockey routines while speeding along on Dexedrine. He had a habit of raising and lowering the volume on the music in the booth which drove Hicks nuts. His right foot would be pumping and his upper body would sway and bob with the rhythms of the music. He was in perpetual motion. Most disc jockeys had one or more of these nervous habits while working.

"It seemed to me he indulged in one drug and another most of the time," Hicks said. "He was kinda radio's Hunter Thompson. It wasn't anything that was strange to us because we were probably doing it too, but not quite as much."

Hicks liked Bobby's style. He said, "Bobby had this conversation with himself thang. He'd say something, and then he'd answer himself. That was kinda cool."

But what caught my attention while talking with Hicks was the story he told about listening to Bobby's show on the radio from home one late night after he'd become a Bobby fan. "He was back announcing some tunes and he says 'that was...I don't know who the fuck it was'. And I thought, this guy has just cooked himself. He just cooked his career."

In fact, Bobby did cook himself but not over scatological language over the broadcast airwaves. His lifestyle simply caught up with him.

Norma was "The Rose of Richmond." Carmelita was "The Knockout of SanFrancisco."

Telegram

LA148

L LLJ116 XLT2616 FS PDB=LOS ANGELES CALIF 20 135P PST=

BOBBY. CARE RADIO STATION KGBS=

338 SOUTH WESTERN AVE LOSA=

THANKS FOR THE "HELLO" ON THE AIR LAST NIGHT. WHAT A PLEASURE IT IS TO HAVE A SUPER-JOCK BACK IN LOS ANGELES. EVEN MY RADIOS GLOWING. PLEASE KEEP IN TOUCHM WITH MUCH LOVE=

PHIL SPECTOR=

(246).

WU 1201 (R 5-69)

27 Ramblin' Round

"My name is...Jesus...Sax Goldberg and the Tutors."

Getting a gig at KSFO was Bobby's dream job and in 1969 he lost it.

"It was the same thing, man. If I didn't get sleep and it was hard to get sleep when you kept taking pills to wake you up. Nobody sounded drunker than I did when I reached that point where I knew it was trouble. I'm not drunk. My name is…Jesus…Sax Goldberg and the Tutors."

Bobby had already been warned about his behavior. He called Al Newman 4-hours before his show and told him that he'd not been able to sleep, that he would pay out of his own pocket to have his engineer, Jerry Thompson do his show.

"Newman said, hey why don't you just forget about doin' it altogether," Bobby recalled. "Of course I got pissed…well, fuck you man."

And that was it. Bobby was again dangling in the world with no job and no prospects.

But there was always "Big Daddy." "Tom Donahue took it as a personal affront that I would be out of work," Bobby said. In the winter of 1969 Bobby tried his hand, part time, at Donahue's KSAN-FM.

"I never felt comfortable workin' KSAN," Bobby said. "I never felt comfortable playin' that music. You never heard anything but the big artists like Eric Clapton, Dylan, Beatles, Stones, Led Zepplin. They were all unbelievably talented people...God, man...incredible. But then along came Grand Funk. The first time I heard them was in 1969. Somebody called and they apologized for asking me to play Grand Funk. I played it and...aw man, what the hell is this? Even Ralph Gleason, in a column for Rolling Stone, tried to explain away the Grand Funk Railroad, man."

Bobby did manage to hook some shows focused on the "Roots of Rock 'n Roll," a chance to play some of the music he liked. But Bobby said that music wasn't why people were listening. "They were listening for the music that was a contemporary of their life," as he put it. "People like what the hell they like."

KSAN kept Bobby in pin money until the spring of 1970 when KGBS in Los Angeles called and Bobby was southern California bound...again.

I too, was unemployed and living in San Francisco at the time and drove Bobby to L.A. in the dead of night. I remember the trip because it was so unremarkable. Bobby and I barely exchanged a word along the way. He was down and I was used to that. It was a comfortable silence but I knew he wasn't happy. What I discovered once we arrived in L.A. was that I was the one who wasn't happy. Bobby was fine without a job. I was not. I was depressed and Bobby was trying to pull me out of it. As I rambled about my sorry state of affairs, I vividly recall Bobby saying to me, "You think too much." And that's what I do. Hearing Bobby say it got me into the moment, we laughed, got drunk and went to see a Sam and Dave performance. It was a great night.

I headed back to San Francisco. Bobby dissolved into L.A. nightlife and his widening circle of friends and fans. He landed a job at KGBS – working with Bob Morgan – a fan of Bobby's since he first heard his show on KFWB. "He was one of my mentors," Morgan said. "I shall always be grateful to him for passing on that incredible strange sense of humor to me. I never met anyone in the industry who had more of a feeling for the music than Bobby. He did not just play the music, he listened to it."

The program director at KGBS, Ron Martin, at first allowed Bobby to pick his own music. Bob Morgan recalls Bobby playing *Beginnings* off the Chicago album before anyone else would touch it. "When KRLA put it on their playlist, Bobby dropped it," Morgan said. It was one of Bobby's great pleasures – breaking a hit record then moving on to the next.

Shortly after taking the job at KGBS, Bobby received a telegram: "It said how great it was to hear the world's greatest disc jockey back on the air in Los Angeles. It was signed by Phil Spector," Bobby said. "When I showed it to the program director he wanted to put it in an ad."

"One night on the air at KGBS," Bobby recalled, "I happened to mention a guy whose name is Sonny Curtis, who was a country and western guy and an incredible song writer. He wrote the opening theme song for the Mary Tyler Moore Show. He had an album…*Beatle Hits Flamenco Style.* It was on imperial records. I mentioned it on the air saying I used to have a copy and don't know what the heck I did with it. I'm not kiddin', thirty minutes later there's a guy at the door downstairs with a package for me. It was from Phil Spector and it was this fuckin' album, man; one of the most obscure albums in life."

"See, I don't use my head. I should have said, Phil I would love to have a copy of everything you have recorded including the Christmas Album."

Bobby again was hangin' at Tommy LiPuma's place where, as Tommy put it, "Music was everything. That's what you got up for. That's what you went to bed with."

That was the fun part. The KGBS part was rapidly getting to be like a job. And for Bobby, that meant red flags. Norma was down by this time and one morning in early 1970, at their converted garage apartment that Bobby called a "shoebox," a few blocks from LiPuma's place, Bobby and his friend Abe Kesh decided to "shoot up" just once. And they figured their best chance would be to do it with Gabor Szabo, because he was a known heroin user.

Gabor Szabo was a gifted guitar player, born in Budapest, Hungary whose work with Lena Horne, Ron Carter, Chico Hamilton, Santana and Gary McFarland caught Bobby's attention in 1966 when Bobby was at the San Francisco middle of the road station, KFRC. Bobby soon became friends with Gabor Szabo and would go see him whenever he came to town.

"I just loved Gabor Szabo," Bobby said. "He was the sweetest, most mellow cat you wanted to protect. I don't know what from, but you knew he was gonna die young, and he did. And I know it was fuckin' drugs. We were very close friends."

Bobby only mentioned the incident quickly in passing, but Norma remembered the day like it was yesterday.

"Gabor came over and immediately asked if I would go to the store and get some ginger ale. I was a little upset about this because, I too, wanted to try shooting up," Norma said. "When I got back, I knew it was too late. Gabor, who had arrived looking ill, was now hopping from stack to stack of records asking if he could hear more Les Paul. He looked better and sharper than I'd ever seen him. Abe, on the other hand, was lying on the couch with his head in a large shopping bag, puking. And Bobby was standing stiff as a board, sweat pouring off his head and trying not to get sick. He did not make it."

"So, Gabor and I had a great time listening to records while Bobby and Abe struggled to stay cool," Norma said. "I found out later that Gabor was very reluctant to shoot the guys up and especially did not want the responsibility of shooting me. That's why he sent me to the store. Twelve years later, Gabor died of a 'mysterious blood disorder' and twenty two years later, Bobby was diagnosed with Hepatitis C. That was the one and only time Bobby ever shot up, so we knew exactly where and from whom he got the HEP C."

Gabor Szabo was among many of the artists – including Bobby Womack, George Benson, Arthur Adams, Mickey Newberry, Bob Dorough and others – who Bobby loved and touted to Tommy LiPuma, Bob Krasnow and Don Graham for their Blue Thumb label. In fact, LiPuma had signed most of these artists to his label about three years after Bobby had mentioned them, eventually following Bobby's advice.

When Tommy was to meet Barbra Streisand for the first time because she was considering him as a potential producer of her next album, Tommy called Bobby and according to Norma, said, 'hey man I'm meeting Streisand next week and need some songs'. Bobby immediately left for LA with Stevie Wonder's *All in Love is Fair* under his arm. Tommy presented the song and two others to Streisand and called Bobby back and said 'That was the one she liked, babe.' It also won them a Grammy.

In the late 70's Tommy did hire Bobby as a music consultant when Tommy returned to A&M as president of Horizon Records. Bobby, I'm told, was elated. His job was to send Tommy cassettes and songs and Bobby would get a check for $200 dollars a week. Bobby told me how close he and Tommy were, how he'd send songs to Tommy that he thought he could use and how very good Tommy was at what he did. "When I heard the guy speak publicly for the first time, I almost died," Bobby said. "He was so polished. It was incredible. Did you ever see him on the Grammy Awards the night he won?" That was Bobby; always a kind word.

Norma, of course, was the strength behind Bobby. She was confident, assertive and totally committed to Bobby. She kept telling Bobby he needed an agent. He kept telling her, "What am I going to do with an agent? I can't even make money for myself." Norma was desperate for Bobby. She wanted the best for him. She felt it was a crime that Bobby wasn't acknowledged and paid for his music genius.

Bobby looked at money, power and prestige differently. He always liked having money but was never in love with the idea of having a lot of it.

Bobby said, "As my mother would say to me when I was leaving the door with my little suitcase and a map of the United States...point me in the general direction of

New Orleans. It's only 1,300 miles through the winter. She said, 'how will you live? How will you eat?' I said, oh I don't know, somebody will buy me something. They always do. Then I said, you got any money?"

Bobby was surrounded by "friends" with money and although he'd never say it, Bobby felt some of them owed him for the advice and airplay he gave them. Bobby never asked for money unless he badly needed it, which was often.

He asked Phil Spector to lend him $500 dollars for help getting him back to San Francisco. Phil said yes, and then didn't show up to meet Bobby at his mansion off Sunset. "Our relationship ended rather badly with me screaming at him: 'hey you little mother-fucker', through the gates of his estate."

Four months later, Phil Spector's secretary called asking Bobby for his address so she could send a check from Phil to Bobby. "I said, tell that fuck face to take the check and stick it up his ass," Bobby said. "The chick never said a word. Whatever I said she kept asking for my address. I gave it to her and I got a check from Phil for $500 dollars. I was floored. And then the car I bought from Tommy LiPuma suddenly needed a valve job which came to $497 dollars."

Bobby liked to tell the story of an engineer at K-SAN whose kid went to school with one of Bobby's sons, Tommy. Bobby went to pick up Tommy one day at the engineer's house. Bobby said, "This guy's got a house you would get lost in. I mean it looked like a fuckin' airport. I knock on the door and I can hear this woman walkin' across a hardwood floor…for an hour…until she got to the door. I said I'm here to pick up my reluctant son, Tommy. And Tommy's the one that's always saying to Norma – but not in a mad way – 'how come if Papa knows everybody in the fuckin' world and everybody knows him, why doesn't he have any money?' I said, well kid that's the breaks. I never got a break in sho biz. That'll be the title. I never got a break. Give me a break."

"I never got a break. Give me a break."

Oh, I didn't tell you that Norma and Bobby were married and had two children – boys. They did…and that will happen when Bobby returns to San Francisco after tying up loose ends in L.A.

28 Life Turns

"Didn't you get suspicious when you found them in bed together?"

The job at KGBS was a record breaker for a short duration, from February to July of 1970. Being on the air in the nation's second largest radio market had its allure and having been told he could pick his own music was just frosting on the cake.

KHJ Radio was now in the Top 40 game having debuted in 1965 with "Boss Jocks" and a Drake formula for chipping away at the KFWB and KRLA rock 'n roll audiences.

Roger Christian was one of those original "Boss Jocks" who'd crossed the picket line with Bobby at KFWB during the strike and worked the all night shift. Roger remained with KFWB until '65, went with Drake at KHJ, but returned to KFWB two years later when the station was owned by Westinghouse. I was there at the same time working the all night shift.

Like hundreds of others, I'd always dreamed of being on the air at KFWB. Dreams come true.

The Westinghouse plan was to change the format of KFWB to all news which it is to this day. The week before the switch, KFWB – after a long period of low ratings – had climbed back to number two in the market.

The staff begged and pleaded with management to not make the switch to all news. It was to no avail. In March of 1968, KFWB's

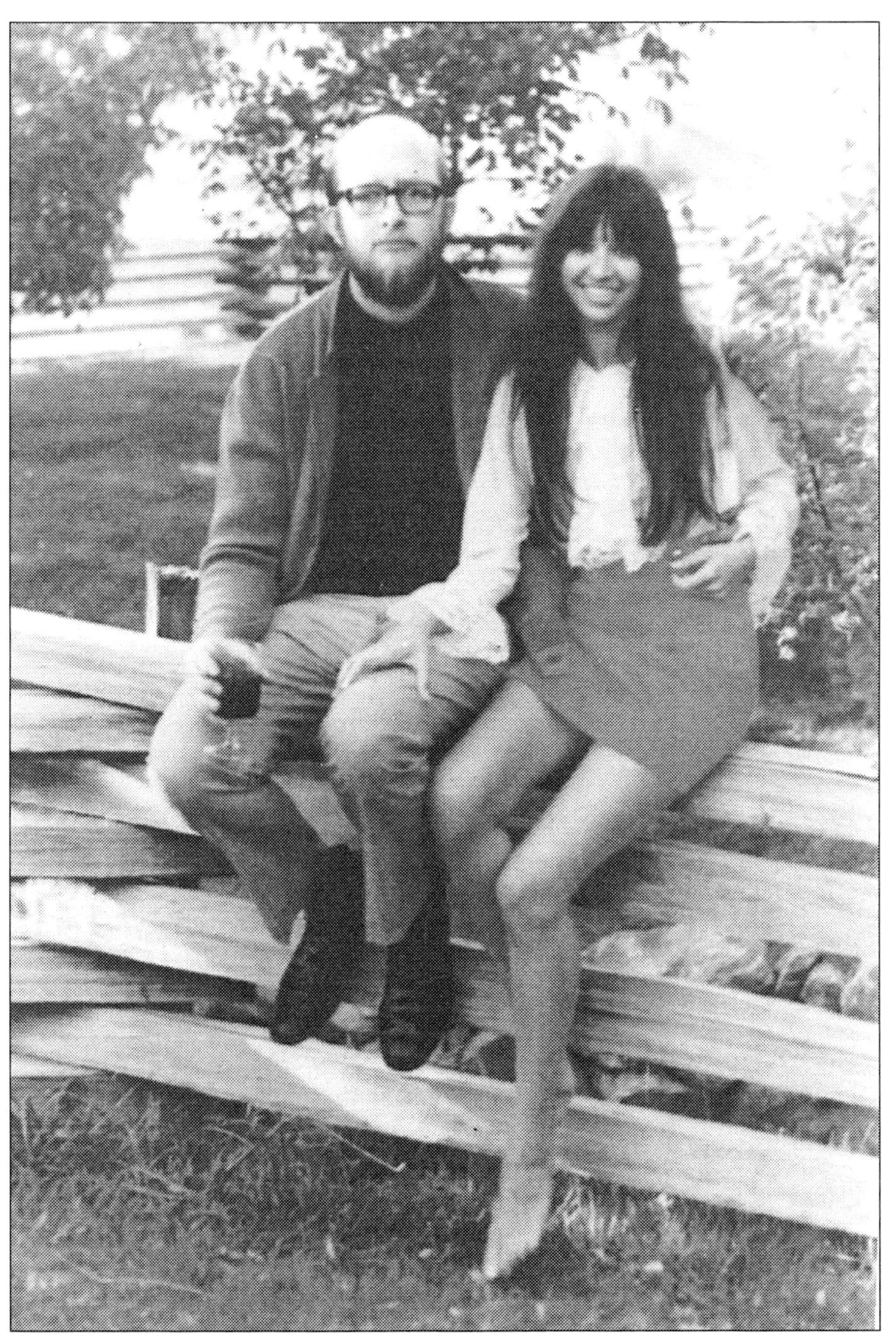

Bobby and Norma – frowns and smiles.

long and legendary music past ended and it has been reported that on that day Roger Christian was reduced to tears. It was more than a change in format; it was the end of an era. By 1970, Roger Christian was working again with Bobby at KGBS.

After work, Bobby and Norma would hang out at the home of "Humble Harv" Miller – one of the "Boss Jocks" at KHJ. "Harvey Miller came from Chile," Bobby said, "And when I met him he was very skeptical of me. He'd heard so many Bobby Dale stories and wondered whether any of them were true. Harvey's wife Gladys completely fell in love with Normi. She just thought Normi was the cutest, best gal that life ever produced, and Gladys was not a warm person. I mean really…she wasn't."

One night, Harvey showed Bobby his record collection in the garage; 500 albums on a shelf. He pulled a Little Richard album and gave it to Bobby. A couple of years later, a paranoid Harvey insinuated that Bobby had gained access to his record collection. Bobby never had.

But what was most interesting at the Miller household was the drama inside that was slowly unfolding like a bad soap opera.

Bobby recalls his nights spent at Harvey's house after Martoni's closed. "We would be there using…whatever the hell…Amyl Nitrate…you name it," Bobby said, "Until 5:30, 6 o'clock in the morning. Then we'd go home. It was a very unusual situation. Anytime I went to Humble Harv's house, Stan Bly was there and Harvey's old lady, Gladys was there. Stan Bly was a sharp guy, a promoter for Mercury records but one of those cocksmen whose whole life seemed to be spent tryin' to get laid. Now I never said anything, but I thought god this must be one of those sophisticated Hollywood marriages, ya know? And it wasn't that way at all."

Norma had a better handle on what was going on. "Gladys was balling Stan," she said. "And Harv was balling the neighbor. Eventually the neighbor got it in her head that if she told Harv about Gladys, and everyone knew but him, he would divorce her and marry the neighbor. Wrong."

Bobby said, "Humble Harv couldn't believe it when he found out that Bly was sleeping with his wife. I almost said, didn't you get suspicious when you found them in bed together? They were never apart. They were like newlyweds."

It dawned on a Saturday night. Bobby was high on acid when Harvey came into the house. Bobby said he looked like a man in shock.

"That's definitely what it was because he'd found out this terrible thing," Bobby said.

"I just about said my god Harv, I've never been here when he wasn't here. He said well he's my friend and friends don't do that. I said, when sex rears its ugly head, I can't remember too many friendships that could hold up to it. I said look at the bright side, you won't have to pay alimony."

For Harvey Miller, there was no bright side. The following Monday morning back in San Francisco, Bobby was stopped on the street by a jock named Frank Perry who worked for Drake.

"He said, Bobby guess what happened in LA. I said don't tell me it was Harvey. And he said how in gods name did you know. I said I didn't know but that I was with Harvey on Saturday night and it was like tryin' to talk to a dead man. It was not penetrating. All Harvey could think of was the betrayal."

Harvey Miller had killed his wife, Gladys – shot her six times - and then had taken a shotgun and was waiting in the bushes where Stan Bly lived, to do away with him. Bly somehow got wind of it and took off for Chicago.

Harvey Miller went to the men's prison at Chino and later sent a letter to Bobby. He wrote: "I don't quite understand how you got one of my records," and expressed concern over his collection. It was the first thing he mentioned. At the bottom of the letter, after serving two years in Chino, California's medium security prison for men, was written: "I'd rather not go into what it's been like in this place, but I can tell you that I've experienced more pain and loneliness than I ever thought existed in this world. It's a continuing nightmare...one long open wound. I've discovered depression on a scale that even you couldn't comprehend. There are no words for it; just raw pain. It can't be described, it can only be experienced. Sincerely, Harvey."

"All Harvey could think of was the betrayal."

A few years later, Bobby got word that Roger Christian had committed suicide. "Roger did himself in," Bobby said. "I said anybody who could write the lyrics to *Don't Worry Baby*, as dumb as they are...it was my favorite Beach Boys record. He wrote that. He wrote for Jan and Dean with Gary Usher. He wrote a lot of car songs. He was a very weird guy."

The Top 40 era drew out the weird guys alright; the very talented, the creative, the hustlers, the fakers, the insecure, the inflated egos and hotheads. They were all very weird and as Bobby once said, "They almost had to be." And Bobby, who passed among them, was probably the weirdest of the bunch. But through the triumphs and tragedies a single theme emerged: it was fun, thrilling in its own way and even when you were down and out, sick and tired, you wanted back in.

I asked Bobby, so if you had it to do all over again? "Oh, I'd be there in a minute. The only thing I wouldn't do is cross the picket line."

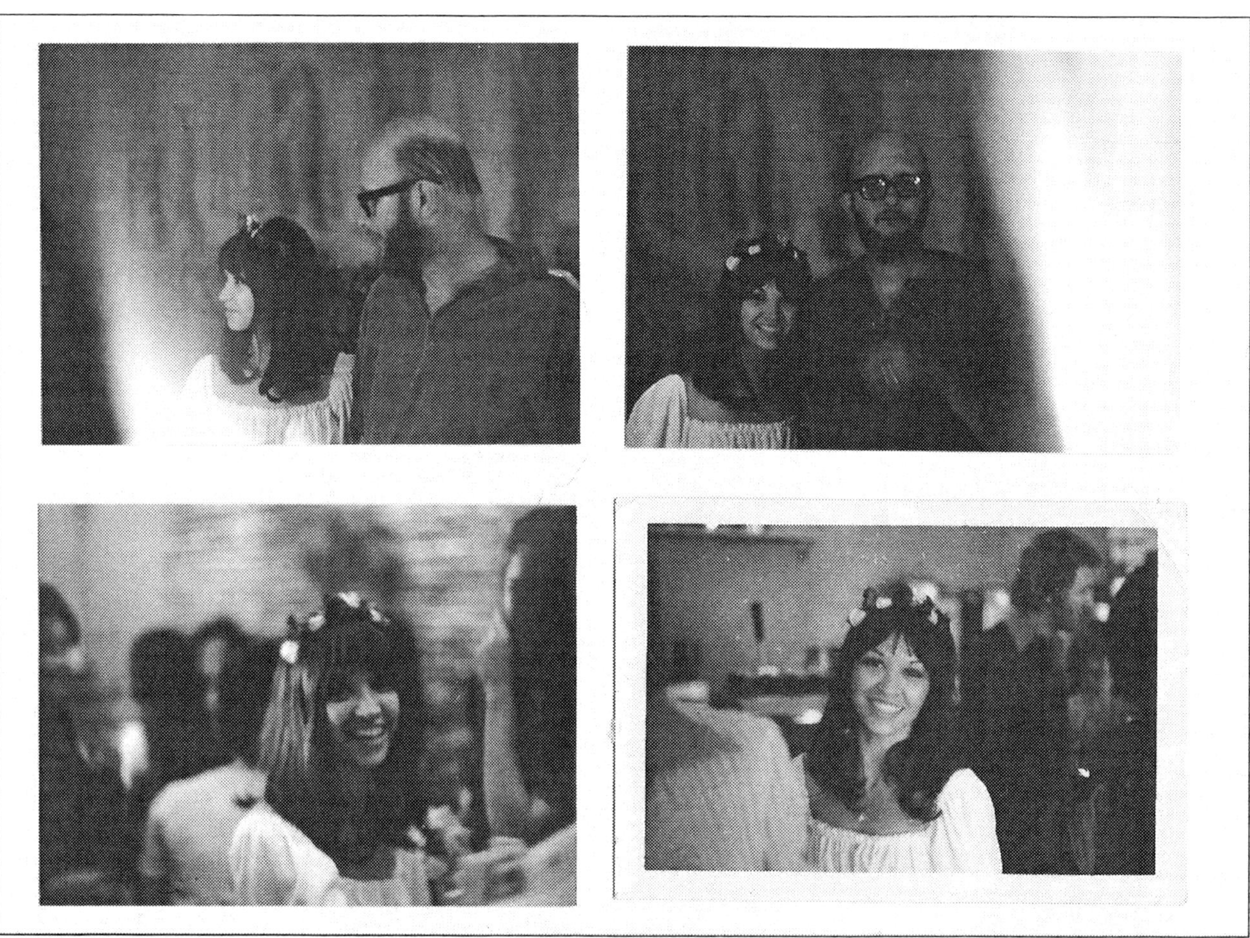

29 Wedding Bells

A personal appearance Bobby couldn't avoid.

"You really missed a truly nice man."

Bobby quit his job at KGBS in LA for a simple reason; the program director hinted, at the urging of the General Manager, that Bobby might want to play a few songs from the stations playlist. Bobby declined.

Robert W. Morgan said, "When the GM at KGBS started putting guidelines down for his show, he said he was leaving and he did. I came to work one night and he was gone. For those who never heard Bobby Dale, you really missed one of the true personalities of Los Angeles radio. For those of you who never got to know him, you really missed a truly nice man."

Even though Bobby told Morgan he never liked southern California anyway, he stayed on for a time in LA waiting for serendipity and living the life of music from great, chemically induced heights.

"Tommy would come over and pick me up in his little Mercedes and go over to Blue Thumb to make his calls," Bobby said.

Bobby would accompany Tommy into the studio on occasions to watch him work as producer for George Benson, Gabor Szabo and others.

When he first went to KGBS, Bobby and a friend, Rick Swigg joined Tommy in a recording session with Dave Mason for the *Alone Together* album.

"Rick Swigg's parents owned the Fairmont Hotels," Bobby said, "Obviously a kid with a ton of money. But he came to LA and he slept on our couch in this horrible little apartment that Normi and I were living in off Western Avenue. I checked with Tommy to be sure I could bring Rick Swigg and we took a cab to the studio. Swigg graciously let me pay for the cab…the fucker, man. I said no wonder the guy's got money."

Tommy was producing the *Alone Together* album and when it was done, had given Bobby a test pressing. "And then I got a call from Tommy in a panic," Bobby said. "Dave Mason found out and Tommy said Bobby I can't have you play the album. Dave Mason was the most paranoid mother fucker I ever saw in my life, man. He was one of those artists who was never satisfied with his work… it could be improved…it could be better. So I gave the album back. No problem."

Bobby suggested that giving the album to whatever FM station "was making all the noise in LA" was a much better idea and Tommy agreed.

"The only thing I regret," he said, was not making a copy of that test pressing while I had it, because it was a different version of that same album when it later came out."

After a few months of Martoni's, music and the drama at Harv Miller's House of blue lights, Bobby moved back to San Francisco where he first got the news about Harvey Miller's shocking crime of passion and in the spring of 1971 Bobby got his chance to do it all over again…at KSFO.

"Never again do I want to hear Bobby's name."

His number one fan there, Pete Scott, talked Al Newman into rehiring Bobby for the weekends. Norma told me she and Bobby were hoping it would turn into a full time gig, but that Bobby was considered a "loose cannon" and that the station really never knew what to do with him. When the front office stayed up late listening to Bobby…they loved him. But he was so unlike their other jocks that they figured the only place for which he was best suited was the middle of the night.

Although disappointed at not getting on full time, Bobby did seem happy to be back in the Bay area with his friends Tom Donahue and Abe Kesh. Tommy LiPuma would fly up on weekends and Enrico's was open every night…late.

KSFO was important to Bobby. He remembered when Al Newman fired him the first time and later said "never again do I want to hear Bobby's name mentioned on KSFO." Apparently after Bobby got fired, other KSFO jocks would say they were turned onto the record they had just played by Bobby Dale. Al Newman would have none of it. But it was hard to stay mad at Bobby and when they met again Newman asked if there were hard feelings. Bobby told Newman he was the guy that hired him and that there was no way he harbored any

ill feelings. Bobby was back where he belonged, playing the best music San Francisco had ever heard in the middle of the night and having his life run by Tom Donahue .

"Tom had taken over my life," Bobby said. "He was a great producer, director. He was the one who got me to grow a beard. He looked at me and said 'you need to grow a beard, Bobby'. I said why. He said 'cuz you'll look better. I said really? He said I'm pretty sure. So I grew one and I loved it."

Norma Milanese, the "Rose of Richmond" – otherwise known to Bobby's listening fans as, Carmelita, organized Bobby's life and was his constant companion.

It was during this second run at the "World's Greatest Radio Station" that Carmelita began taping Bobby's programs. She electronically gathered up an audio file of Bobby's best and worst radio performances. She made deals with Tower Records for the tapes and cassettes and spent hours not only supervising the actual taping but logging the tapes with notations of what was happening in their lives at the time. Her catalogue is extensive including out-of-print album cuts, European imports, performances by Bobby on those acid enhanced, happy days and those down and out days; the good, the bad and the ugly.

I have copies of those tapes. Norma would send them to me periodically. And when Bobby would tell me the stories of his life he would recall specific airchecks to highlight the mood at the time. One such story was one, those of us who knew him well, were surprised to hear; the decision to remarry.

"I never met a woman like Norma in my entire life."

"If you couldn't make it with Norma…as far as getting along with someone…then there is no point in doing anything," Bobby said. So, I just thought…what the hell…she really wanted to get married. I never met a woman like Norma in my entire life…that was as good as her. The thing is I didn't want kids again, man. And when they did come everything changed."

But let's not get ahead of ourselves.

Norma's recollection of the wedding proposal goes something like this: "We had been floating for weeks on 'Blue Heavens', a synthetic mescaline. We were in Abe's pool in Sleepy Hollow when Bobby suddenly says, "What do you think about getting married? When I asked why, he said because I have nothing to lose and everything to gain."

That was August 16, 1972 and Norma said once Bobby had made his proposal he seemed to want it over as quickly as possible. They went to Enrico to ask if the wedding could be performed at his place. He not only agreed but offered to pay for the event and asked Ward Dunham, the bartender at Enrico's if he would do the invitations.

At about the same time Bobby had been sitting in for Russ the Moose Syracuse on KSFO's all night show and when Scott Beach relieved him at 6am, he told Bobby he'd heard about the wedding plans and offered to perform the ceremony saying he was ordained in The Universal Life Church. Bobby accepted. And that's when trouble started.

Tom Donahue got wind of it, called Bobby and was hurt that Bobby and Norma hadn't asked him to marry them because he, too, was ordained by the Universal Life Church. Donahue did not take this perceived rejection well and pouted inconsolably. Bobby reacted badly and began referring to Donahue as "Tom Dominant" – on the air.

In the run up to the wedding, Bobby was working a two week stretch of overnights and taking copious amounts of speed and acid. He was pissed at Donahue, angry with columnist Herb Caen for not posting his wedding announcement – calling him Herbie Caen on the air. And I would venture that a state of high anxiety began taking hold as "wedding day" approached.

The day of the wedding – September 8, 1972 – Scott Beach, who was to perform the ceremony at 2pm that day informed Bobby that he would be late. Beach had been chosen Lord Mayor of the Renaissance Festival and had to make a personal appearance and could Bobby and Norma delay the ceremony until 5pm. They could not.

Plan B was, of course, Tom Donahue. Bobby called and explained the situation and amid references to being "number two" Donahue relented and officiated at the wedding later that day.

"I don't know how he talked her into it."

It was a crowded and lively affair including guests from LA and points east. I attended with my new girlfriend, Marty, but we stayed on the sidelines – observers of this spectacle. Having worked with Bobby the year he got married the first time in Minneapolis and knowing how he felt about the institution, after hearing about the planned nuptials, I had to see it with my own eyes.

The irony was Enrico's; this famous spot in North Beach where, if you were ever out "Bobby Dale Hunting," you would find him. And there we were, celebrating Bobby and Norma's wedding...in a bar...Bobby's favorite place on the planet. And it was Bobby Dale's biggest personal appearance ever. He showed up and I'd never seen him happier.

There'd always been talk of the age disparity. Bobby was 17 years Norma's senior. She was born the year Bobby graduated from high school. Even Norma's father, "a sweet man" Bobby called him, was uncomfortable with the age difference.

But two forces were indisputably at work. Norma was obsessed with Bobby Dale and Bobby, although he loved Norma to death, was strongly attracted to young women.

"I was never a big fan of *I Want to Hold Your Hand* by the Beatles," Bobby said. Maybe it was the fact you heard it so goddamn much, but I loved the other side; (singing) She was just 17, you know what I mean... (laughter) ...Tom and I agreed on that. That's it, man."

It was inevitable that Bobby and Norma's age difference would create whispers.

"That's the funny thing," Bobby said. "One night, I was workin' with Norma on a weekend...it was a Sunday. There were a couple of gals who worked at KSFO and they were out in the lobby talking and they didn't know I was in the hall. This is when Normi and I were gonna get married...and I heard the gals talking...'I don't know how he talked her into it'...ya know? I thought, how weird 'cuz this isn't how things were at all."

It started with a chocolate cake when she was 14 years old and told her skeptical girlfriend she was going to marry Bobby Dale. And now at 23 this determined young woman was in for the ride of her life.

There was no honeymoon. "We never traveled," Norma said, "except in our heads."

Music and drugs would consume their lives, often with tragic consequences. Norma would much later recall, "Sometimes we were so high that the air passing through my nose felt ice cold. I could almost see it. Now, I sometimes feel that drugs robbed me of my youth, dreams and ambitions. I feel I could have gone so far if I had been straight and gone to school or gotten a job in radio myself, or modeling.

Gillie LiPuma, Tommy's wife and Norma's best friend once told Norma she knew how much Norma loved Bobby but said if you play your cards right you could be living in a mansion in Brentwood.

At over 400 pounds, Tom 'Big Daddy' Donahue's philosophy: "Everything to excess."

Norma said, "I knew she was right, but I know I would not have traded my life with Bobby for any of that. There was no way I could have left Bobby, even though I knew I would never have anything material from a life with him."

One thing was certain. Norma Dale would never live a life of regrets. She chose an emotional roller coaster that would give her pleasure and pain.

30 Friends and Fate

"The stroke left him like a 12-year-old child."

Abe "Voco" Kesh – the man who knew more about music than Bobby Dale and one of Bobby's closest friends – produced an album with various artists called *Lights Out* on the Blue Thumb label, Tommy LiPuma's label.

Bobby played the album religiously on KSFO. You actually do get by with a little help from your friends. And Abe Kesh was the first of Bobby's close friends Norma met. He lived in a "hippy style" studio apartment above the Filbert Street Stairs. It contained a king size bed in an alcove of the one room. Norma said, "The bed had all kinds of blankets on it, including a fuzzy one, sort of synthetic fur. It sat in front of bay windows where lots of votive candles had been placed on the window ledges, along with a small candy jar filled with Swedish Fish."

Bobby had called Norma asking her to take a cab over to Abe's place where he had been taking acid and smoking hash. Bobby offered Norma a hit of acid – Owsley's White Lightning she recalls.

"I knew Bobby would never offer me anything that would hurt me," Norma said, "and because I trusted him completely, I took the biggest piece and swallowed it. Bobby looked horrified and said 'you took the biggest piece. You probably won't be able to move for a while'. He rolled his eyes and placed a bunch of pillows all around me and put the first set of headphones I had ever tried on my head. Suddenly, *Sgt. Pepper's Lonely Hearts Club Band* exploded in my ears and while listening to Jimi Hendrix's *Axis Bold as Love*, I really thought Jimi was in my head, walking from one side to the other, whispering in my ears. It was an incredible trip."

When Abe finally came home and "grumbled" as Norma recalls, at seeing Norma and her sister sprawled in his bed and his jar of Swedish Fish devoured, Norma got to know the man she would later declare "was like a brother to me."

Norma learned that day that Bobby and Abe were always in competition for control of the turntable. That first day Abe got in his licks with Albert King's *Born Under a Bad Sign* album and followed it with Junior Wells' *It's My Life Baby* and *Stomach Ache*. Norma recalls it vividly.

Norma loved weekends with Abe. After the Friday, all night at KSFO, Norma and Bobby would head for home. Abe would be there and Norma would cook breakfast.

"We'd watch the Bugs Bunny Show and whatever sports came afterwards," Norma fondly recalled. "In between all this, Bobby and Abe would play records for me while I lay zonked on the couch. I loved when they started playing Woody Herman with both telling stories about members of the band. It was like they were showing off for me."

By now Abe was calling Norma, "NJ" for Norma Jean, and she and Bobby began sleeping at Abe's place on Friday nights, get up for the Saturday night show at KSFO, return to Abe's to watch Notre Dame highlights.

In early 1973, Abe ended up in Marin General Hospital with a severe case of kidney stones. What Bobby and Norma didn't know was that Abe had been suffering from kidney stones for some time and had been taking Percodan and heroin to control the pain. In the hospital, morphine was the drug of choice and it was there Abe suffered a major stroke and brain damage.

"The stroke left him like a 12-year-old child," Norma said.

Bobby and Norma tried to care for Abe in their Oakland home but before long, Abe became incontinent and often non-functional. "Bobby decided that he couldn't do it anymore," Norma said. "Seeing Abe like that was too depressing for him. So we had to cut Abe out of our lives. That is something I never would have done myself, but that's the way Bobby was. If he couldn't handle something, he'd block it out one way or the other."

Many years had passed when word came that Abe had died of a heart attack in 1989.

Voco's "turntable hit" in San Francisco, courtesy of Bobby Dale.

On April 18, 1975, Bobby received a letter from the KSFO program director: "Dear Bobby: It is my unhappy responsibility to advise you that effective this date, your services are no longer required by KSFO."

The official reason for firing Bobby was that he "Falsified the log": entering a public affairs program as having run on two occasions when, in fact, it had not.

Bobby knew the simpler version, "They wanted me off the air."

In fact there was a firing frenzy going on. Gene Autry had sold the controlling interest in KSFO to Signal Oil and by mid '74 house cleaning had begun from the top down.

Bobby said, "They got rid of everybody. We killed that family. They were a very good station…KSFO. They were stability. There were no guarantees but that was as close as you'd come to a guarantee…that this station would go on and on."

Bobby's first instinct was to talk to Tom Donahue about what was happening. He never got the chance.

31 Alone Together

"Bobby felt there was no chance of him ever working in radio again."

Tom Donahue died of a heart attack April 28, 1975, 10 days after Bobby's firing. Donahue was a rock in Bobby's life. Bobby told me, "I not only lost a dear friend when Tom died, I lost an employment agency."

Donahue was a San Francisco institution, a towering influence in the radio and music industry. And at his "Irishman's wake" at the Orphanage – a once popular and successful Rock Club – he was eulogized in somber but outsized ways, surrounded by the radio "celebrities" he'd made possible and musicians he'd made famous.

Van Morrison, Dan Hicks and Peter Yarrow were among the many recording stars providing the music. And the bar was open.

Dusty Street was there, one of the stars of KSAN, the radio station that had become Donahue's lasting success story and indelible weave in the fabric of San Francisco.

Bobby Dale was there, the man whose life had been taken over by Tom Donahue, the man who was described by Donahue as "A sniper above the freeway," the man who'd become "Big Daddy's" constant companion.

And Abe Kesh was there…physically. Abe didn't recognize Bobby or Norma. It was all too much for Bobby and he began to spiral into a very deep depression.

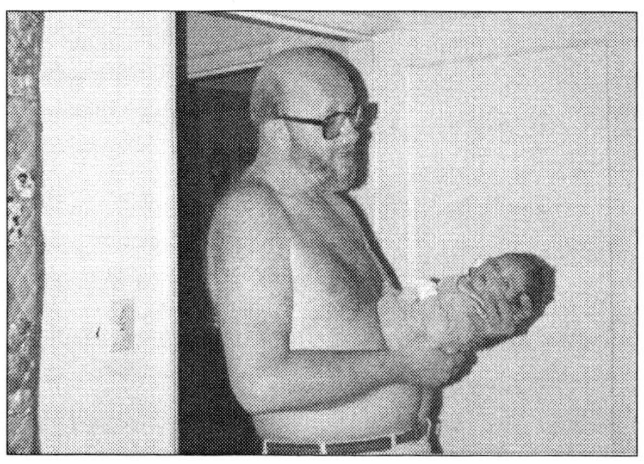

The marriage ended when the children came.

As Norma remembers it, "Bobby felt there was no chance of him ever working in radio again. He spent months in bed on heavy downer drugs. It was a very scary and lonely time for me. At first I tried to keep up with him, taking Quaaludes, Placidyls or Thorazine, drugs my pill doctor gave us for getting down off acid."

Keeping up with Bobby proved to be a life saver for Norma. She became extremely sick, recognized the symptoms of OD'ing and got off the pills. Her drug taking days dwindled. But Bobby was another story. Norma told me that she thought, during this time, that if Bobby had been a stronger person he would have committed suicide.

"Bobby never thought he would live to be 40," Norma said. "He was surprised to be alive at 36 when we first started living together. I didn't think he would make it either. He did everything to excess; too many uppers at one time, too many downers, alcohol, no sleep...you name it. Sometimes it felt like we were adrift at sea on a tiny raft in the middle of a terrible storm. It was scary."

Norma began to doubt herself. Was she doing the right thing for Bobby? Should she continue to support, comfort and hide him away or set him free?

And while the loneliness closed in on Norma like a thick fog across San Francisco Bay...Bobby slept. His radio career was over, his friend Tom Donahue was dead, Abe Kesh didn't know him and Tommy LiPuma was too busy. And this time, the phone didn't ring with offers of work like it used to.

Bobby kept hoping that his friends in high places would reach out and give him a hand, help him get a job. No one did.

When the storm broke, Norma's dreams began to change. She was bone tired of working to keep them afloat and decided to stop working for a year. Since age 19 she'd made good money as a data processing supervisor or lead operator.

Bobby stole record albums from Tower Records to pay the rent. While in radio they'd been getting albums from "the boys" in the store, in exchange for uppers and downers, but Norma said, "this became a bigger thing. "We needed food, rent, bills, etc." Bobby began appearing from time to time on the University of San Francisco campus radio station, KUSF.

But Bobby and Norma moved to Richmond to save on the rent and in July of 1982 Norma, who told me she was desperate to have a baby, gave birth to a boy, Joey.

The day after Joey was born Bobby got a call from a former KYA jock named Norman Davis. Bobby had been out of work for 5 years at the time.

"Norman was hired at a little daytime station in the City of San Raphael called KTIM," Bobby said. "It was his idea to do a big band kind of format. He asked if I'd be interested. He said there's no money to speak of...but if you want to be on the air again. I said, hell yeah, that'd be great. And it was a gas; nuthin' but Fats Waller and Louis Armstrong... ya know? Woody Herman...all these old jazz records I remember from being a kid."

At home with a child to take care of, Bobby and Norma's marriage began to wither.

Norma said, "Bobby worked afternoons at KTIM that went off the air at sundown. This meant while I worked 9 to 5, Bobby would watch baby Joey in the mornings, drop him at daycare, go to work and come home. I thought things were going well until I found out that by the time Joey was two, Bobby had put together a couple six-hour videotapes of cartoons that he would put in the recorder and sit little Joey in front of the TV with his little lunchbox, and then go back to bed and read. By the time Joey was three and allergic to everything, Bobby had secretly started smoking again and Joey was a wreck. When the doctor asked if anything had changed in his little life, he volunteered, 'Papa's smoking again'."

KTIM was an AM/FM operation. Bobby worked AM with a weak daytime signal that was strong only in the east bay and difficult to sell. And when a new owner moved in, Bobby moved out and decided to ride out his unemployment and hope for the best.

Norma had been on maternity leave with a second son, Tommy, who was born in July of 1986. When Bobby got the news that

"Too many uppers...too many downers."

KTIM had been sold, Norma immediately got a job as a receptionist in a law firm. She trained as a legal secretary and earned five raises in five months but still not enough to pay off credit cards because Bobby's unemployment check couldn't cover it.

"Even before I conceived Tommy, I knew the marriage was over," Norma said. Bobby couldn't or wouldn't adjust to life with children, and didn't like being second on my list. He wanted to be able to hide in his room when he wanted to be alone, and suddenly I couldn't do everything by myself. I needed help."

Help came in a second phone call from Norman Davis. He'd gotten himself and Bobby gigs at KKCY – an easy listening rock station in San Francisco nicknamed "The City."

"It had been a punk rock station, if you can believe that," Bobby said. "Oh god, you should have seen the guys working there. They were the scuzziest slime balls that you've ever seen in your life. Just unbelievable. In fact, the night before they were to turn the station over to the new owners, they pissed all over the control board; 10, 20 thousand dollars damage. It was bad. The station was called "The Quake," mostly punk rock, Sid Vicious and all that shit."

But the "The Quake" became "The City" with a manager who had been a salesman at KSFO and wanted Bobby for the all night show and then the seven to midnight show. The station began to do very well in the ratings and the sales staff made the most of it, inundating the station with commercials.

Bobby said, "That's one thing I'll say for Drake, man...he really did it the right way. Instead of raising the number of commercials, he raised the rates because he had the ratings."

What Bobby didn't know was that the new owners of the station wanted to get ratings up in order to sell the station for a big profit, which is what happened. Bobby was again out of work in early '88. "It was really an example of what happens when you deregulate because now radio was like used cars." Bobby said.

At home the day of reckoning came just before Mother's Day, 1988. The kids were sick. The house was a mess and Bobby was in the bedroom with the door closed, reading. Norma asked him to give her a hand. He did so, grudgingly, madly vacuuming and tossing litter into the fireplace, burning it.

On Mother's Day morning, 5-year-old Joey asked Norma the whereabouts of the bag he'd brought home from kindergarten containing the mother's day present he had made for her. Norma said, "That's when I realized Bobby must have accidentally grabbed it and threw it in the fire. That did it. I asked Bobby to leave later that night, and all he said was, 'can I stay until Thursday when I get my next check'?"

When I talked at length with Bobby 12 years later, he was matter-of-fact about the split with Norma, his "punkin."

"I knew the marriage was over."

"I didn't want kids," Bobby said, "and naturally when they did come, everything changed. It's like in one of those "Frazier's." He's talkin' to somebody on the phone about making love and the guy said we're gonna have a baby. And Frazier said, 'well making love won't be much of a problem any more' and then he said, 'you can trust me on this one'. But, it's true."

Bobby acknowledged that Norma had grown up, become a mother and that her boys had become the most important people in her life. Bobby accepted that and went on his way.

But some things never change and Bobby's lifestyle was chief among them. He smoked three packs of Kool Regulars a day, popped pills and acid when he could afford them and consumed more alcohol then ever.

After his all night shift, he'd stop for drinks at a workingman's bar on Union Street. He would marvel that just after 6am there'd be 15 or 20 people already knocking 'em back.

Bobby had listened to one of his old shows and after the 5 o'clock news heard himself say, "Another hour of the Bobby Dale show – something to do before the bars open." At 6am he'd head for the bar. "There was a pretty big crowd for 6am," Bobby said. "They were all on their way to work, belting down screwdrivers and heading out the door by seven in the morning."

Bobby would be left alone in the bar, his workday was over.

"That was the life in radio," Bobby said, "especially in markets like up here. My god, if you drank a lot up here, you were nothing. You need to drink more. This is a terrible place for people who had drinking problems. I obviously had one because I would get blackouts. "I woke up one morning in a fuckin' closet. I could smell moth balls, man. I was on the floor of a closet in an apartment that I didn't know who the fuck lived there. I came walking out of this on a Saturday morning and here are these girls having breakfast at this table, and they screamed. I said good morning, excuse me, I'm just passing through here and I walked out of the place."

Bobby's love affair with alcohol was a problem shared with others of his family. His sister Janie was a heavy drinker and his brother Pete has been in Alcoholics Anonymous since the 60's. Bobby told me his oldest brother was a problem drinker, but that Pete was worse. "He was an alcoholic and made no bones about it," Bobby said.

Pete began getting a handle on his alcoholism after a trip to see Bobby in LA in the 60's. Tommy LiPuma took Pete to see the movie *Days of Wine and Roses.* "That did it for Pete," Bobby said. "That fuckin' movie, for an alcoholic – not drunk at that time – it had a tremendous impact on him."

The last I'd seen of Bobby Dale was at his wedding at Enrico's in 1973 by which time

Bobby, big sister Janie, Norma and the boys.

I'd already made the transition to television. And by 1980 I'd relocated in Atlanta and become part of CNN's original news team, working as an anchor and correspondent.

I remembered Bobby often, each time I played a favorite album he'd taught me to appreciate or reminisced about my radio days and careless ways. He taught me a lot. He was an important person in my life and I felt saddened that I couldn't have lived closer and gotten to know him better. Since I'd not heard from him or about him, I'd imagined that he'd abused himself to death.

I was CNN's prime time anchorman on August 17, 1989. It was 8:04pm eastern when we got word from our sports crew, getting ready to cover the third game of the World Series between the Oakland Athletics and San Francisco Giants, that there'd been an earthquake. And it was only minutes before we learned how serious it was.

Our first pictures were at the stadium where the game was getting underway, but shortly every television camera in the Bay Area was turned on and rolling in all directions producing America's first major earthquake broadcast live on television. The reporting was like peeling the layers of an onion, as word spread of the damage. Part of the Bay Bridge had collapsed, freeways had buckled, homes destroyed and cars tossed like playthings. We went wall to wall and several hours later when I was relieved on the anchor set, it was decided I'd take a producer and crew and fly to San Francisco in the morning to cover events on the ground in the aftermath. It was a big story for days.

"I was on the floor of a closet."

We were on the first jet allowed to land at San Francisco Airport after the quake and headed for the Marina District – one of the most devastated residential areas – and set up shop. It was my job to appear on camera every hour with stories of how people were affected by the quake. And there were plenty of them. Parts of the Marina district were leveled, people had died, some miraculously survived, homes reduced to splinters and rubble, even more homes destroyed and condemned – their owners allowed in for only minutes to gather a few treasures – photographs, stuffed animals… a favorite pillow.

After that first day with still no power in the much of the city, we headed for our hotel and were issued small flashlights to guide our way to the rooms where we were treated to ice cold showers and an uneasy night of light sleep punctuated with aftershocks.

We did it all again the next day and when we returned to our hotel, the power was on and we were exhausted. I surfed for music on the bedside radio and found a station playing some great jazz. I relaxed. The song ended and the hoarse voice told me the name of the song and said: "This is Bobby Dale." I nearly fell out of bed.

I tracked down the station and called, not expecting an answer because it was after midnight. Bobby did answer and told me he'd been watching my reporting earlier in the day. In fact, he said he watched me all the time and praised my work. I considered it a high compliment.

I took a cab to the station, was greeted with a hug – a first – and it was as though no time had passed. Bobby seemed truly happy to see me and I was, of course, amazed that we'd reconnected in this most unexpected way.

With his jazz music draped in the speakers around us, we talked into the night, interrupted by only brief disc jockey duties. Brief because Bobby's voice was going and he said he didn't know why. I said the Kool Regular he was spinning in his right hand might have something to do with it. But, again, some things never change and except for the raspy voice, Bobby was what he was. He was funny, we talked about "the good old days" we shared as radio people often do. We exchanged phone numbers even though I never expected to hear from him. And I left; content that Bobby had not died without saying goodbye, Bobby looked very sad when he waved and locked the door behind me.

A short while later my Atlanta phone rang. It was Bobby. He needed money for a throat operation. His years of taking amphetamines had taken their toll on the nodules in his throat – had dried them out and made it harder and harder for him to talk – not a good thing for a guy earning a living in radio. About the pill taking, Bobby said, "If you wanna hang in there for the whole ride, it's always best to use a little moderation." I sent the money and urged Bobby to keep in touch, that I didn't want him out of my life.

In fact, over the next ten years it was Norma who arranged for Bobby to stay in my life by having him reflect on his own life in phone calls between us. The last six months of his life we spoke every day and I took notes. He'd never been more animated. He was open and seemed happier than I ever heard him. He, in fact, looked forward to our daily chats, to my delight.

Norma had remained in close touch with Bobby. To know him was to love him. She moved within a few miles of Bobby knowing that he'd make no effort to see his sons if it was too much an effort. Bobby did make the effort and near the end of his life our daily 2-hour conversations would end when it was time for Bobby to pick up his son Tommy at school.

"I love to get my kid because he's a gas," Bobby said.

Norma had also played the major role in reconciling Bobby with his boys by suggesting romps in a nearby park, The Civic Center Lagoon. It was the first time Bobby had been to a park with the boys and brought along a bag of bread to feed the ducks. Over the next few years, Bobby taught the boys to make little fishing poles out of sticks and string. They put globs of bread on the end, no hooks, and

"I love to get my kid becasue he's a gas."

tried to catch fish and sometimes they did.

Norma said, "I had always known that Bobby would make a great father, but it took me years to realize he would only be able to be a part time father. He could never give all of himself to anything or anyone."

Bobby began developing a closer bond with his oldest boy, Joey by having him stay overnight with him on weekends at a place he was living with two other guys.

And suddenly, again without looking, Bobby landed another job. This time it was back to the future at the station where he'd last worked – KKCY, "The City." It had new call letters, KOFY, and a new owner, Jim Gabbert – a notorious San Francisco media player with big plans for his radio station and it had nothing to do with radio.

Bobby was hired to do overnights. It was the station where Bobby and I reconnected after the '89 Loma Prieta Earthquake. It was the last radio job Bobby would ever have and it ended after Jim Gabbert's tumultuous tenure. Gabbert wanted a "soft rock" station but he had to strike a deal with a large group of listeners who petitioned the FCC to keep the format as it was when KKCY was becoming increasingly popular in the community. Legal documents were signed. Gabbert ignored them, paid a fine and did as he pleased. He softened the format and began firing disc jockeys one at a time.

"He was an interesting guy for real," Bobby said. "Him and his lover were Stanford graduates and Gabbert, when he came out of the closet, everybody really cracked up, because we all knew he was gay. Why would you come out of the closet? He would have his meeting and all the jocks would be there and – this really happened. He said, 'I'll tell you this. If everybody's show sounded like Bobby Dale's we would not have to have these meetings. And one month later…he fired me, man. You knew if he cheered for you, you were in big trouble."

Gabbert then sold the radio station to Viacom and parlayed the cash into the purchase of TV Channel 20 in San Francisco. KOFY, Bobby Dale and all the others were just pawns in the big game. Radio was becoming computerized, homogenized and no longer in need of outstanding talent. You had to pay for that.

Bobby's radio days were over. And his life was in jeopardy.

32 Paying the Piper

"It's your liver and you don't want it hanging over your belt."

When preparing for the operation on his voice box, tests revealed that Bobby had diabetes, a heart problem and cirrhosis of the liver.

Bobby had become aware of what alcohol was doing to his body in the early 60's when Tommy LiPuma sent him to a doctor, that just so happened to be the father of singer, songwriter, Randy Newman. Randy was a close friend of Tommy's and Bobby had run into him frequently at Tommy's house. Bobby hadn't gone to a doctor in all his life, and now he knew the time had come.

Bobby said, "I made an appointment with Randy's dad and he said 'I understand you know my son'. 'How is Mr. Showbiz'? Well, I said, he's kinda the same, sorta screwed up. Talk about shy people. Randy, it took him a day and a half to get him outta the closet... and he was straight."

"I'm getting this physical," Bobby recalled. "Randy's dad said gimme your hand and he puts it under my rib cage and says feel that? I said what the hell is that? He said, 'it's your liver and you don't want it hanging over your belt. He said, 'one more drink or one more cigarette and you're going to die'."

It was the siren sound. Bobby began leading the semi-straight life, cutting down on booze and adding milk to his scotch.

"The straight life is a fuckin' drag," Bobby said. "I'd like to go to a fuckin' bar and watch a football game. But I can't. I don't like to go to bars when I don't drink. It's like being around drunk people and it's a drag."

Bobby was also about to become homeless. The two guys he was staying with were moving to Santa Rosa and two days before they were to make the move, Bobby got a phone call from his ex-girlfriend, Judy Briscoe. She'd seen Bobby walking in San Rafael, called him and offered her guest room to him while he rearranged his life. Bobby was very grateful but had only two weeks to find his own place because Judy's mother was coming to visit from Arizona. He responded to an ad in the Independent Journal: "wanted – male in his early 60's to be a grandfather at a pre-school." Bobby was told if he wanted the job, it was his except it paid no money. But, they said, you have an air conditioned apartment upstairs at the school.

"I would be there when school opened in the morning, mothers would pull up to let their kids out and I would hand them a clipboard and make them sign their kids in. Many of the mothers were very young and very incredible looking. I mean people with money always smelled better."

Bobby would set up equipment for play time and help with "snack time." "Which was the roughest," Bobby said, "because you came in and you tried to show these kids how to pour nectar or lemonade. They would have that and a cookie about 10:15."

I was actually a bit stunned when Bobby told me this story. This hip, bohemian, funnyman whose radio talents had record promoters at his feet was now being called "Grandfather Bob" by a hoard of squealing preschoolers.

I asked Bobby if he learned something about himself because of the experience. Ever on guard, he answered, "I learned it's a lot nicer to have a place to sleep."

After we chuckled over that, Bobby did reveal something of himself, "When you think about it, there's nothing more valuable or precious in the life of people than their little kids. Ya know, they come and they drop them off at this little place...and it's kinda scary."

Bobby also renewed his part time fatherhood by entertaining his own kids, Joey and Tommy, showing them around the school and communicating the only way he knew how.

"The Simpsons was always the biggest link between me and my boys," Bobby said. "As far as communicating, the biggest breakthrough would be the Simpsons; I have probably 40 tapes of their shows. My oldest boy about a year ago asked if I still had the one where Montgomery Burns runs for office. I told him, god yes, that is my favorite. It's the one where they're fishing and the investigative reporter goes to interview them and they catch a fish that has three eyes. Everybody panics because the fishing hole is right below the power plant – that nuclear plant."

I asked Bobby if he felt close to his boys since I knew he felt great guilt over his oldest son with Carol that he completely ignored.

"Best thing in my life," he said. "Absolutely. You remember what Homer said: 'if it wasn't for your face Bart, I wouldn't make it through the day."

Bobby began another review of his life on his visit to the Social Security office. He said, "They handed me this little piece of paper. It looked like half a page of a paperback and on it in this infinitesimal small print…every job I ever worked in my life. It went on forever. Three weeks at so and so. Another week and I'd have had seniority, man. Oh, Jesus, what a fuckin' life."

When asked if he had children, he was told they'd get $750 dollars a month between them as child support payments. Bobby would get a little over $600 dollars a month. Not a lot but Bobby had lived on less and now he was also contributing to his sons' upbringing and he felt good about that. So how, you ask, do you live on $600 dollars a month?

There was a teacher at the Junior School. She was in her 70's but "a real groovy gal" to use Bobby's words. "She said Bobby you got to start goin' to the Whistle Stop. It's only a dollar-and-a-half for a hot meal that is really good. It's a nice place and just a few blocks away."

The Whistle Stop is a senior center that used to be the train depot in San Rafael and looks the same on the outside as in the 40's when it was a stop along the Marin Railroad.

Inside there were English classes for immigrants and all manner of activity on behalf of older folks. And the food was good.

Meanwhile back at the pre-school, Grandfather Bob, now sporting his own sweat-shirt with "Grandfather Bob" stitched on the front, was getting worn down.

"It got too much after awhile," he said. "I mean trying to control…if it had been all little girls it would have been no problem…but my god man…boys are…I said this is terrible. These kids should not be allowed to live."

Bobby always identified with W.C. Fields who once said, "Children should neither be seen or heard from – ever again."

"One day I'm in the yard and I asked this cute little girl, who are you? She said I'm one of Patrick's babes. These kids are not even 5. I had to break up a sex ring back in the Teddy Bear House. This girl from a broken home and her mother belonged to a commune where everybody obviously slept with everybody else. And this little girl said she was showing boys how she would like to have them blow on her stomach. I'm thinkin' wait a minute…how old do you have to be, man?"

Bobby's energy was beginning to flag and he needed more peace and quiet and he found it in a 20 x 15 studio apartment with a small kitchen featuring an empty refrigerator for $187 dollars a month.

"It's the size of a shoebox," Bobby said. "It's subsidized housing. Ya know, I'm old and I'm broke. Course, it's my fault. I'll be 70 in July. That sounds really old, man. It does until I go to the Whistle Stop – 'young man come over here. Give me my milk. I mean, they're seniors. They do a lot of bitchin' baby."

Bobby hated getting old. "It's a fuckin' drag," he said. "I remember Jack Carney, a jock at KSFO, telling me he was on vacation somewhere. He was walkin' down the street and he sees this old guy coming toward him. Then he realized he was seeing his reflection in a store window and the old guy was him. He went out and bought the best fuckin' wig he could find. The Rolling Stones knew what they were talking about in that famous song, *What a Drag it is Growin' Old*."

Despite his editorials on life and growing older, Bobby seemed content in what he considered his old age.

"I have my little studio," he said. "I have enough money to pay the rent and my job at the Whistle Stop takes care of my food."

The Whistle Stop Senior Center was within walking distance and Bobby would go there every day to help manage the midday meal for 30 to 40 older folks who come because they have a very limited income or they seek companionship.

"I hand out milk to the ladies," Bobby said. "After all, that's 80-percent of who's there. All the men are dead and the women are alive. There's something weird here."

After the meal is served, Bobby helped with cleanup and getting the old folks on their way. Some required help with a wheelchair. "My day then is spent praying he doesn't have to go to the bathroom before it's time for him to go back on the bus," Bobby said. "Tryin' to get that wheelchair in there…you'll have to hold it Joe…sit there with your legs crossed."

Bobby hated that part of the job.

Bobby spent most of his day in his apartment which was littered with clothes, audio tapes piled high and video tapes everywhere; on chairs, tables, stereo, TV and most liberally on the floor. He was always taping *The Simpson's* and all football games good or bad. Norma said all offers to help him clean up the mess were turned down. He kept saying he would get to it.

One wall of the apartment was nearly all window looking out over a beautiful rose garden, stone pathways and a cherry blossom tree that sprang to life in brilliant pink in the spring.

There was a bed and a small shelf stacked with some of his favorite books: *Citizen Hearst*, *Studs Lonigan*, *The Lindberg Trial*, *The Rising Sun*, *Blind Faith*, a few *World War Two* pictorial history books, a couple *Simpson* books and a variety of old Look magazines he purchased at a collectors store at the Northgate Mall.

On a side table/dresser, Bobby kept pictures of his boys and Tom Donahue. Another framed photo of Donahue hung in the kitchen with a photo of himself with Elvis Presley hung alongside.

This was what was left of Bobby's world. He preferred being there alone listening to tapes of his KSFO shows and Norma told me for a man who didn't want his shows taped in the first place, he truly enjoyed them in the last 3 years of his life.

Bobby said, "It pisses me off when I listen to some of my old shows. If I would have just taken the time to listen to them while they were being done, I would have corrected so many things that were annoying little habits, ya know? Like talking over the records and just in general...showing up." But Bobby did enjoy the music. The only music he listened to was on those old tapes. His album collection he'd already given away.

Bobby also spent considerable time looking after his old friend, Herb Kennedy, an old news guy who worked with Bobby at KSFO. Herb was in a nursing home and Bobby made it a point to stay in touch.

"He's just a sweet guy," Bobby said. "He lives in this little nursing like home I guess, and I try to get out there every other week. And I always keep in touch. I call him 3...4 times a week. I'm his only contact with the fuckin' world. His wife has never forgiven him for being the vodka drinker that he was, which came as a big surprise to me. I thought this guy when I knew him...that he was one of those guys who pulls his news shift and goes home. Then I find out he was never there sober. From the time he got up in the morning, he'd belt down vodka. And I'm thinkin', Jesus, how can you do that and do the fuckin' news."

"It pisses me off when I listen to some of my old shows."

Two days after Christmas in 2000 Norma took Bobby to the hospital for a CT scan leaving Joey at Bobby's place on the pretense that he was to wait for the cable guy. Joey had his instructions from mom and spent the morning straightening up the messy room, throwing open the drapes and when Bobby returned to his gray little room, depressed over results of the scan, it was bathed in sunlight and there was Joey beaming with his arms wide open getting a hug and a kiss from his proud dad.

Norma and a girlfriend finished the job. It took many hours. But after putting things away, rearranging furniture and photos and cleaning every nook and cranny, Bobby was delighted with his home and eager to have guests.

He did not, however, ever listen to another of his shows because Norma had put them all away.

Bobby then told me about the CT scan and what it meant.

Photo: Jim Marshall

Among Bobby Dale's biggest fans were elite members of the recording industry. In this rare photo, Bobby receives a kiss on the head from Jerry Wexler, the legendary producer who gave us hits by Ray Charles, Aretha Franklin, Wilson Pickett, Dusty Springfield and Bob Dylan. They called Wexler, the man who invented rhythm and blues.

Smile. OK. That'll work.

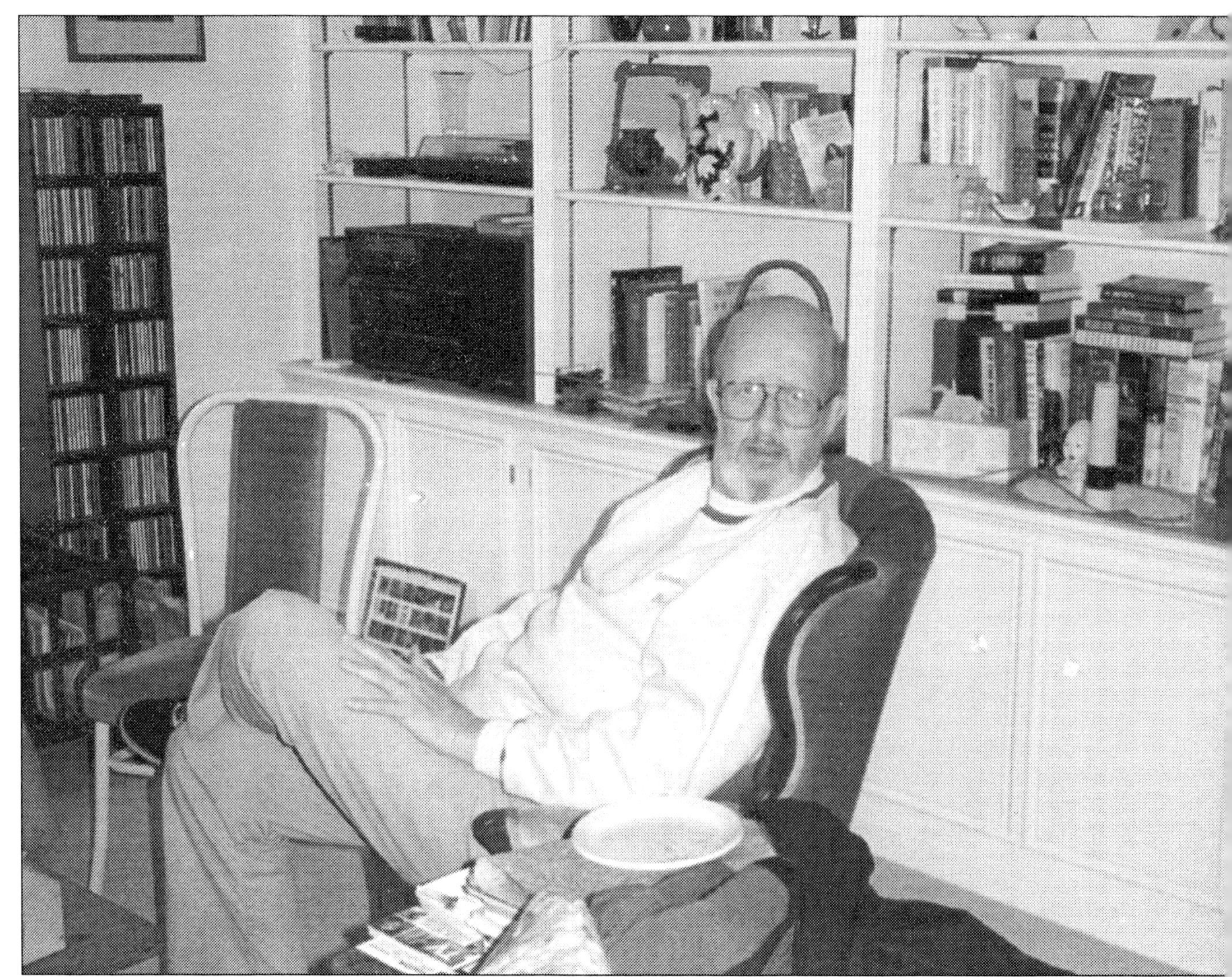

33 Last Words

"I have two months to live."

"Well, reality is what it is," Bobby said, "I have two months to live…at the most. And that's being generous. It makes me sad. But I do have Norma. She stayed here last night. We shacked up. God, it was something having that little baby doll around."

Tommy LiPuma flew in to see Bobby. His first, Best Man, Charlie Boone showed up on his doorstep, I was on the line everyday at Bobby's insistence. Another friend, Ron Lyons, was with Bobby the day a guy from the medical service delivered a shower chair. Ron called it a 'fitting memory of the Bobby I knew'. "The buzzer sounded," Ron said. "Bobby could barely sign the receipt and as he was writing the delivery guy looked at the wall, saw Bobby's pictures and said, 'Hey, I know you. I've listened to you'. After he left, I turned to Bobby and said, 'You never get tired of that shit, do you?' And Bobby replied, 'No, man. He was just workin' me for the tip."

It was a painful ending for Bobby but the remarkable thing was he immediately accepted his fate. He told Ron Lyons, "When they tell you it's over, it's over."

Bobby told me, "When I look at my wasted life and realize that even if things had been different they would have happened the same way anyway. I would never have been any different."

He would have been in his room listening to classical music when he was a boy. His brother, Pete called it "strange and lovely music" and when he asked about it, Bobby looked up and said it was Scheherazade by Rimsky-Korsakov. Pete said, "I never got over that. It was so Minneapolis – a hard working middle class to poor family…and classical music."

He'd no doubt go to church with his mother – not for the religion which he thought was weird, but for the music. "Oh, I loved some of the hymns, man," Bobby said. Remember the Gene Ammons album – *Preachin'*? This was an album he did when he was in jail for doin' drugs. He had gotten busted too many times and he did *Holy, Holy, Holy* and *Sweet Hour of Prayer* – just him and an organ player. It was a beautiful album. I really liked that."

If he had it to do over, Bobby would still play an out of print RCA album on the radio called *Folk Favorites* by Sam Cooke and spend mornings at Aldo's in Hollywood having coffee with him.

Cooke told Bobby he was the only person he ever met that even knew about the album – *Grandfather's Clock* was a staple of Sam Cooke's in-person act. Bobby said, "He never did a show without doin' that damn song. If you listen to the lyrics and the way he would sing these things, they were quite different from what people thought they were."

"I asked Elvis if he wanted to do a hop."

Bobby would most certainly choose to goof with "The King," the second time around. He would poke fun on the radio at KFWB and then get a call from Elvis telling him, "I heard that." Bobby said, "One night on the air I said, Jesus I'm tired of this guy and all these records. And Elvis was in his limousine, man…and heard it."

Elvis got a chance to sample Bobby's humor when Colonel Parker was persuaded to allow Bobby onto the set of *Girls, Girls, Girls,* the latest "epic" film, Elvis called it.

"I didn't know it was a big deal," Bobby said. "Any other jock would have notified columnists, newspapers…yeah right. I didn't do any of this stuff. So I asked Elvis if he wanted to do a hop."

Bobby had his photo taken with Elvis – the same photo that ended up on the wall of his "shoebox" apartment in San Rafael alongside the photo of Tom Donahue.

Bobby said, "When Norma showed that photo to Joey – my eighteen year old – he looked at it and said, 'Am I supposed to know these people? And Normi says, 'Jesus, that's your dad, the one on the left' ya know?"

But for all the stories of Bobby Dale, recognized as one of America's top 100 disc jockeys in a special exhibit at the Rock 'n Roll

Hall of Fame in Cleveland, this guarded urban legend who probably agreed with W.C. Fields that, "if I had to live my life over, I'd live over a saloon," said his fondest memory was of the farm in Iowa.

"It was such a big part of my life, I can't tell ya how big a part it was," Bobby said. "I don't know why. Maybe it was just suddenly being on a farm where all this farm machinery was...going fishing for catfish. Ya know...it was just incredible."

"I'll never forget. It must have been about 1945...and it was my mother, my brother and myself. We had to take a cab and we missed the fuckin' train, man. So rather than go all the way back to our house in South Minneapolis, my mother said: well, we'll just stay here until the other train leaves about 7 o'clock at night.

This was about 10:30 in the morning. So she gave my brother and me some money and we went to a couple of movies and wandered around...then came back and caught this train at night...which was a big treat. When we arrived in this little town of Clarion...which is where we would be picked up...of course, the people on the farm, they did not have a phone so there was no way to get ahold of them.

They must have shown up to pick us up and we weren't there. They just went back home. And so we got off the train about 2:00 in the morning and, of course, this is a little town of maybe 10,000 people. I don't think there was a single thing open in that town. But it was so nice and warm and we sat in the park. And my brother and I were running around swinging (chuckle), teeter tottering...doing all this shit...but it was one of those beautiful warm nights...and no mosquitoes man because you didn't have lakes in Iowa like you did in Minnesota.

And then we caught a train...a milk run train...at 6 o'clock in the morning that took us to a little town of about a 100 people called, Holmes, Iowa. And from there we could walk up to one of our relatives and then everybody was so surprised to see us. And they took us over to the farm that we stayed at – Mervin and Selma's place."

We drove the tractors, helped out on the farm; it was really a big part of my life."

Pete remembers those days at the farm as, "My fondest childhood memories." He recalls loading bales of hay. "Man did we work," he said. "We loaded the bales onto a flat bed wagon and rushed back to the barn, all the while seeing the dark ominous skies closing in."

Mervin taught the boys to fish and hunt. They'd head out at night, turn the headlights on and shoot pheasants when they popped up. Pete said, "After dinner we'd sit out on a big cement slab, near a cellar door and Mervin would reach in his shirt pocket and pull out a bag of Bull Durham. It was the enchanted moment."

Mervin deftly rolled a cigarette and slid a wooden match along his pant leg to light it in a way that Pete considered "pure magic," "a wonder for two young boys from South Minneapolis."

Pete was more demonstrative than Bobby in his tales of those pristine days so close to nature with the kerosene lamps, the shadows and closeness of the animals. He loved the wood burning stove, corn on the cob and night sounds. The silence was deafening. "My god, what an experience," Pete said.

As he was dying, Bobby said, "In just the last few years if I had trouble sleeping, I would lay in the dark and I would picture that farm and this huge oak tree that was in the yard…and the pump house…and the barn where I would go get the cows up from the pasture. It kinda gave me a sense of belonging to this place. In fact, I loved it so much I almost stayed there. I was gonna go to school and live there through the winter."

Bobby fell in love with the haunting and beautiful music of Mickey Newberry, the Texas Singer/Songwriter. "I used to play San Francisco," Mickey said. "Bobby would come. And we'd end up at his house, me and Susie, my wife. We'd listen to music and he'd make me play more songs. He loved music. He never got tired of it. He was the only disc jockey in the United States who played my music."

"One night on the air he played my album three times."

Mickey told me 26-percent of all the records he sold on the Electra label were sold in San Francisco and they were all sold because Bobby started playing the record.

"One night on the air he played my album three times," he said.

It was Mickey's album, *Looks Like Rain*, "He was listening to it when he died; Norma told me he had a physical reaction. Bless his heart. He loved that album."

One night on the air, Bobby said, "Mickey Newberry can bring me down faster than 32 warm beers on a summer night in Minneapolis."

It was a high compliment.

In a coma one morning in January of 2001, Norma played for Bobby, *Looks Like Rain* and Mickey Newberry's haunting and soulful voice spread through Bobby's heart, moved him physically, and sent him on his way.

> *"I don't think much about her no more.*
> *Seldom, if ever, does she cross my mind.*
> *Yesterday's gone but it's better forgotten*
> *like the poisoned red berries that die on*
> *the Vine."*
>
> *- lyrics by Mickey Newberry*

34 Epilogue

"He was a gentle man."

While looking around his bright sunny room in those last days, Bobby said, "God I'd give one hundred dollars for just one nice cloudy day."

Norma had planned "The Bobby Dale Benefit"– a chance for old friends to be with Bobby a last time. It was to be held January 20th from 2 to 5pm at the San Rafael Commons, where Bobby lived. Norma told his friends that Bobby hoped to be there. Three days before the event, Bobby must have decided not to show up. He slipped away when Norma was out of the room.

His friends did gather at the Commons and poured out their hearts for weeks in e-mails posted on the Mickey Newberry chat site.

David Haynes – a record promotion man back in the days and who introduced Bobby to Mickey's *Looks Like Rain* album – wrote: "Today I learned that Bobby had gone to sit in with Count Basie and Lester Young. I know he's blowing riffs upstairs and telling people about good music. He was one of the most wonderful and gentle human beings I have ever known."

Mickey Newberry, himself, wrote: "He was a gentle man with the soul of a rebel…a great sense of humor…and I will miss him."A man named Jeff S. wrote: "One could believe, Mickey, that eternity now possesses

Photo: Ben Fong-Torres

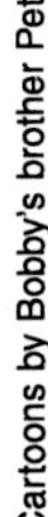
Cartoons by Bobby's brother Pete.

Bobby – a place where time no longer matters. He's probably hearing lyrics you haven't even written yet. One could believe."

Bobby loved his life, but did have regrets. He told me it was no secret to him why he ended up serving food and taking care of older folks down at the Whistle Stop–guilt over the anguish he caused his mother. Bobby did not attend her funeral in '71. He said he just couldn't do it.

Bobby did attend the funeral of his father – the quiet man from Norway who didn't get the chance to celebrate Bobby's career. He was alone nights in Minneapolis trying to dial in Glendive, Montana radio so he could hear his son– happy his boy had found something to do that he loved. He died of a heart attack in 1956.

In his wallet, after he died, Norma found a photograph she thought she had lost. It was the picture of Norma and Bobby the first day they met down in Jack London Square. Norma said, "He had cut it to fit. I had not teased my hair that first time. My hair had gone flat. I felt really ugly when the picture was taken, but because Bobby said he really liked my hair, I never teased it again. I really had it bad."

I asked Bobby if there was a theme song for his life. I was pleasantly surprised when he told me there was. It was a song he couldn't believe I'd ever heard of but, in fact, I'd played it often and it reminded me of Bobby in every way. It always brought tears to my eyes. It's from an album by Ian and Sylvia called *Full Circle.* It includes the song written and sung by Ian Tyson called *Stories He'd Tell*:

Years turn and life turns
Beyond windows and doors.
The life that he lived is not his anymore
But I think of him often
I remember him well
The places he'd take me
The stories he'd tell

-lyrics by Ian Tyson

"He had cut it to fit."

Acknowledgements

Telling Bobby Dale's story would not have been possible without the candid reflections of Bobby Dale himself during the last 6-months of his life.

Because Bobby was often reclusive, those closest to him helped solve mysteries to better understand the life of this very private person. I thank Norma Dale, Bobby's sister Janie, his brother Pete, best childhood pal Jim Watkins, Tommy LiPuma, Johnny Hayes, Sam Sherwood, Judy Briscoe, Raechel Donahue, Dusty Street, Mickey Newberry and Dan Hicks for their invaluable and generous assistance.

A special thanks to Norman Ellis-Flint for creative and spiritual support, and to Tom Morin for his love and dedication to the memory of Bobby Dale thru his attention to detail in the design of this book.